The Viceroy of Ouidah

by the same author

IN PATAGONIA

The Viceroy of Ouidah

BRUCE
CHATWIN

SUMMIT BOOKS
NEW YORK

*Beware and take care
Of the Bight of Benin.
Of the one that comes out
There are forty go in.*

SLAVER'S PROVERB

Copyright © 1980 by Bruce Chatwin
All rights reserved
including the right of reproduction
in whole or in part in any form
Published by SUMMIT BOOKS
A Simon & Schuster Division of Gulf & Western Corporation
Simon & Schuster Building
1230 Avenue of the Americas
New York, New York 10020
SUMMIT BOOKS and colophon are trademarks of Simon & Schuster.
Manufactured in the United States of America
10 9 8 7 6 5 4 3 2 1

Library of Congress Cataloging in Publication Data

Chatwin, C. Bruce
The Viceroy of Ouidah.

1. Benin—Description and travel. 2. Chatwin,
C. Bruce. 3. Sousa, Francisco Félix de, d. 1849.
4. Gezo, King of Dahomey, d. 1858. 5. Ouidah (Benin)
—History. I. Title.
DT541.2.C42   916.6'83   80-17896

ISBN 0-671-41253-1

Preface

In the nineteenth century the Kingdom of Dahomey was a Black Sparta squeezed between the Yoruba tribes of present-day Nigeria and the Ewe tribes of Togo. Her kings had claw marks cut on their temples and were descended from a Princess of Adja-Tado and the leopard who seduced her on the banks of the Mono river. Their people called them 'Dada' which means 'father' in Fon. Their fiercest regiments were female, and their only source of income was the sale of their weaker neighbours.

Abomey was the name of their upland capital. The name of their slave port was Ouidah (spelled Whydah by the British, or Ajuda, meaning 'help', by the Portuguese) — today a forgotten town memorable only for the ruins of three European forts and its temple of Dagbé, the Celestial Python who opened the eyes of Man.

When I first went to Dahomey in 1971, it was still called Dahomey and Cotonou the capital was still a town of belly laughs and French brasseries. Six years later, a new President had changed its name to the People's Republic of Benin, and the fetish priests of Ouidah had put pictures of Lenin amid the scarlet paraphernalia of the Thunder Pantheon.

I had come a second time to collect material for a life of the white Brazilian slave-trader, Francisco Felix de Souza. He came to the Coast in the early 1800s and was stationed at the Portuguese Fort at Ouidah, which, at that time, provided the principal source of manpower for the mines and plantations of Brazil. Somehow he fell foul of the Dahomean king, Adandozan, who took him prisoner to Abomey and had him dipped in a vat of indigo to dye his skin black. (White, in

1

Dahomey, is the colour of death and the immortals: to kill a white man was taboo – and impractical.)

De Souza was rescued from prison by the young prince who later became King Gezo. Some time after the escape, the two men met in the forest and swore a blood pact to help each other. De Souza supplied the firearms for a coup d'état and, in return, received a monopoly over the sale of slaves. By the 1830s he was the richest man in West Africa and the bugbear of the British Abolitionists. He died a ruined man.

All went well with my research until, one Sunday morning, my taxi happened to be travelling in the opposite direction to a plane-load of mercenaries who had landed at Cotonou airport and were shooting their way towards the Presidential Palace. The driver exclaimed, 'C'est la guerre!' and turned the car round, only to fall in with a unit of the Benin Army. I was arrested as a mercenary: the real mercenaries retreated back to the airport and flew off.

The next two days I would prefer to forget. Within a week, however, I had got to Rio de Janeiro, there to follow up the Brazilian aspects of my story – penniless, and with a very sore big toe which a lady corporal had stamped on.

I did not go back to Benin.

I did come away with the bones of the story and a number of vivid impressions. As a boy I had read accounts of King Gezo's Amazons: now I knew what they were like. I had read accounts of human sacrifice by the Victorian travellers, Duncan, Forbes, Burton and Skertchley. I had met Pierre Verger, the master of Afro-Brazilian studies. I had read his essential book, Flux et reflux de la traite des Nègres entre le golfe de Bénin et Bahia de Todos os Santos. *On journeys up and down the Slave Coast I had met De Souza's descendants and carried away an image of his last surviving daughter, a white woman 'as white as you, sir!' Finally, at Abomey, a friend and I called on*

2

Gezo's grandson, Sagbadjou, a vast and aged monarch, who sat on the green plastic seat of his throne and told us what he knew of the Brazilian:

'He was a big man,' he said, 'bigger than the two of you together. My grandfather lifted him over the prison wall. My grandfather, you see, was even bigger than De Souza.'

Such is the background to this book. But such was the patchiness of my material that I decided to change the names of the principal characters – and went on to write a work of the imagination.

March 1980   B. C.

3

ONE

THE FAMILY OF Francisco Manoel da Silva had assembled at Ouidah to honour his memory with a Requiem Mass and dinner. It was the usual suffocating afternoon in March. He had been dead a hundred and seventeen years.

The Mass was said in the Cathedral of the Immaculate Conception, a stuccoed monument to the more severe side of French Catholicism that glared across an expanse of red dirt at the walls, the mud huts and trees of the Python Fetish.

Turkey buzzards drifted in a milky sky. The metallic din of crickets made the heat seem worse. Banana leaves hung in limp ribbons. There was no wind.

Father Olimpío da Silva had come into town from the Séminaire de Saint-Gall. A white-haired presence in a crimson cassock, he stood on the south steps, surveying his relatives through steel-rimmed spectacles and swivelling his luminous bronze head with the authority of a gun-turret.

Not only a priest but an ethnographer by calling, he had attended the lectures of Bergson and Marcel Mauss at the Sorbonne; had published an intricate volume, *Les Sacrifices humains chez les Fons*, and was unable to begin a sentence without a qualifying adverb: '*statistiquement . . . morphologiquement . . .*'

Gravelly organ music floated by; the organist had a limited range of chords.

The Da Silvas had come from Nigeria, from Togo, from Ghana and even from the Ivory Coast. The poor had come by bus and taxi. The rich were in private cars, and the richest of all, Madame Hélène da Silva, better known as Mama Benz, now sat sprawled over the back seat of her cream-coloured Mercedes, cooling herself with a fan of 10,000-franc notes and waiting for the service to end.

Everyone in the family knew their ancestor by his Brazilian name, Dom Francisco.

He came from San Salvador da Bahia in 1812 and, for over thirty years, was the 'best friend' of the King of Dahomey, keeping him supplied with rum, tobacco, finery and the Long Dane guns which were made not in Denmark but in Birmingham.

In return for these favours, he enjoyed the title of Viceroy of Ouidah, a monopoly over the sale of slaves, a cellar of Château Margaux and an inexhaustible seraglio of women. At his death in 1857, he left sixty-three mulatto sons and an unknown quantity of daughters whose ever-darkening progeny, now numberless as grasshoppers, were spread from Luanda to the Latin Quarter. Yet, among those who gathered in the square, only five had travelled to Europe and none to the Americas.

Turbaned ladies hobbled towards the cathedral, scuffing the dust with feet too splayed and calloused to admit the wearing of shoes. Their cottons were printed with leaves and lions and portraits of military dictators. They hauled themselves into the teak pews.

Little girls tripped about in frilly dresses: their hair was balkanized into zones, each zone twirled up in a tinselled plait.

Their brothers wore tight pants and shifted from foot to foot, holding, but not wearing, the red-starred caps of the Jeunes Militants.

8

The younger men were in national costume, the old men in suits of white duck or faded khaki.

The lives of the older Da Silvas were empty and sad. They mourned the Slave Trade as a lost Golden Age when their family was rich, famous and white. They were worn down by rheumatism and the burdens of polygamy. Their skin cracked in the harmattan; then the rains came and tambourined on their caladiums and splashed dados of red mud up the walls of their houses.

Yet they clung to their képis and pith-helmets as they clung to the forms of vanished grandeur. They called themselves 'Brazilians' though they had lost their Portuguese. People slightly blacker than themselves they called 'Blacks'. They called Dahomey 'Dahomey' long after the Head of State had changed its name to Benin. Each hung Dom Francisco's picture among their chromolithographs of saints and the Virgin: through him they felt linked to Eternity.

Father Olimpío rose before the altar and intoned his annual message in a consoling baritone: the Father-of-Them-All had not died but come to Life Everlasting. He looked down on his Children from his Heavenly Resting Place. He counselled them from the infinite store of his wisdom, 'especially,' he added in an undertone, 'in this, your hour of need'.

At the *Credo*, the ladies sighed, heaved their thighs and got to their feet. Letters, lions, leaves and military dictators rustled and recomposed themselves.

Mrs Rosemary da Silva, the wife of a Lagos accountant, shut her ear to the blasphemies: she was a Methodist. She sat when they kneeled for the *Sanctus* and she sat through the *Agnus Dei*. Her husband, Ernest, was beside her, sweating into an English blazer, wishing she hadn't

9

come. He felt a rush of love and pity for his own kind. She merely did her best to embarrass him.

She made a show of adjusting her straw boater. She smoothed the folds of her white piqué dress and clacked three ropes of glass beads against her bosom. When the Da Silvas went up to receive the Host, heads bowed in reverence, she looked airily up at the ceiling, wondering how long it would take to fall down.

The building reeked of decay. Seams of rust were splintering the iron pillars of the aisle. The blue planks of the roof were rotten. Someone had stolen the ivory Dove of Peace inlaid into the altar table. Though the Virgin still beckoned from her niche, her hands were tied in a tangle of cobwebs.

And there were one or two more conspicuous changes: a Red Star hovered over the Crèche; the faces of the Holy Family had been repainted the colour of Balthazar, and the confessional was full of scarlet drums.

After the Benediction, the family sang the canticle *Mi do gbe we (Salve Regina)* in Fon. Father Olimpío slapped his missal shut and small boys scampered for the sunlight.

ON THE STEPS of the cathedral the Da Silvas posed for their annual photograph.

Agostinho-Ezekiel da Silva was in charge of the ritual. A birdlike gentleman of eighty-nine, he was one of the four surviving grandchildren of the Founder, and Head of the Family.

10

His skin stretched tight over a bald and shining skull and his toothless mouth was drawn to a perfect O. Silently, he waved instructions with a silver-headed cane: the old people would sit on chairs, the young would stand on the steps and their parents would fill the space between.

Two spindly boys helped him compose the group. Their names were Modeste and Pierre and they were having a terrible time with the ladies.

'*Mettez-vous là, madame!*'

'*Bougez, madame!*'

'*Ne bougez pas, madame!*'

But the ladies went on fidgeting, arguing, elbowing and shoving their sisters aside.

Nor were the men behaving any better.

Uncle Procopio, a retired flautist of the Dakar Conservatoire, was reciting his 'Ode to the Death of the Dahomean Republic'. Gustave the intellectual told him to shut up. Africo da Silva was describing his gas station. Karl-Heinrich said that Togolese State Railways ran on time, while old Zéférino, a Kardecist medium, spoke of the planchette conversation he had had with his brother, Colonel Tigré da Silva, in exile on the Champs-Élysées: as usual the colonel had been sipping champagne and eyeing the girls.

Meanwhile the photographer was getting desperate.

He was a young man called Cyriaque Cabochichi, with a shaved gourd-like head, skin so black it glinted blue and the most serious approach to his profession. On the back of his sleeveless orange jumpsuit were a purple lamb and letters reading 'Foto Studio Agnew Pascal'.

He stood behind his tripod, half-hidden under the black cloth, signalling with both arms to Modeste and

11

Pierre to push the ladies from either end and squeeze them within the frame of his plate camera.

The boys got wildly excited. They shoved at the ladies' backsides. They slapped them. They pinched them. But the ladies took no notice: their attention was drawn to the Python Temple where a European tourist was photographing the *féticheur*. The old man stood on one leg, a blue cloth round his midriff, pulling a face of absolute contempt, with the python's head nuzzling his left nipple and its tail coiled round his umbilical hernia.

The sun throbbed and slid downwards, casting blood-red shadows and gilding the jagged edges of the papaya leaves.

'The light's going,' moaned Cyriaque Cabochichi, and brought the ladies to their senses.

Nothing was going to deprive them of their photograph. With a show of unity unimaginable a minute before, they turned sideways into a conga and the length of the line shrank.

Papa Agostinho set a picture of Dom Francisco on his knees. His chief wife, Yaya Felicidade, tried to control a wayward breast. Gustave tilted his bowler, Procopio twiddled his moustache. Modeste held up the green satin banner of the Société Brésilienne du Carnaval, and the ladies spread their mouths to the camera: flashes of white and gold burst through their lips.

Overhead the first fruit bats were flying towards the south-east. There was a vague smell of guavas and stale urine. Cyriaque Cabochichi lifted his lens cap and replaced it.

FROM THE PLACE de l'Immaculée Conception the family set off for the Portuguese Fort.

Two boys beat a tam-tam. Smaller boys waved maracas, banged gongs, whirled bicycle tyres, and cartwheeled in the dust. Pierre carried a wreath of pink vinyl roses to place on the shrine of the Virgin.

At the end of the Rue du Monsignor Steinmetz, the procession made a detour round the carcass of a bombax. The Minister of the Interior had declared the tree 'a sorcerers' restaurant' and ordered it to be chopped down after a subaltern of the Gendarmerie caught an old man in the act of nailing a charm to its trunk: the charm had contained a bat claw, some crushed spiders and a newspaper clipping of the President.

The Da Silvas came into the Place du Marché Zobé. Mountainous mammas were sailing home in the opposite direction. Long-fingered Mandingo traders were folding lengths of indigo into tin trunks. The medicine man wrapped the excrement of a rainbow into a rag, and the state lottery salesman was making his final call to the *'fidèles amis de la chance'*.

It was the hour when the fetish priests slaughtered a fowl over Aizan, the Market God, an omphalos of cut stone standing alone in an empty space.

It was also the hour for the intellectuals of Ouidah to gather at the Librairie Moderne and discuss the latest books, even though its stock had been reduced to back numbers of the *La Femme soviétique*; the *Thoughts* of Kim Il-

13

Sung; a Socialist novel called *Le Baobab*; Racine's *Bajazet*; a complete Engels and some pots of macaw-coloured brilliantine.

And it was supper-time. A hundred smoky lamps had lit up the booths where optimistic matrons were ladling millet beer from calabashes, frying fritters in palm-oil, wrapping maize blancmange in banana leaves or grilling joints of agouti, a big rat with yellow teeth.

Their hands reached out for their customers' money – pink, moist and affectionate as dog tongues. Babies were tucked into their cottons. All were asleep: not a single baby cried.

One of the women plucked a wing-feather from a live fowl and twizzled it in her ear.

'It's to take away the human grease,' a small boy informed the European tourist: and the tourist, who was collecting this kind of information, patted the boy's head and gave him a franc.

'I like the Whites,' the boy purred, 'because the Whites repair me.'

Mama Benz went in the Mercedes: she was far too heavy to walk. As the chauffeur drew abreast of the mammas, she stopped for a snack of agouti in sauce, handing out a white enamel bowl to the woman, who handed it back.

The boy said, 'Mama Benz is a carnivore, heh?'

More little boys, teeth glittering in the half-light, kept up a deafening chorus: '*Ago! Yovo! Ago! Yovo!*' – which means, 'Go away, Whitey!'

Meanwhile the Da Silvas turned right up the Rue Lenine, past the Hotel Windsor, past the Hotel Anti-Windsor and came up to the Bar Ennemi du Soir, where Uncle Procopio slipped in for a drink.

14

Nailed to the wall was a rattan mat with three giraffes moving through a Chinese landscape, beside which someone had scrawled in blue chalk:

The dog howls
The caravan goes by

Two Lagos taxis were parked outside, the Confidence Car and Baby Confidence. Earlier in the afternoon the groans of love were heard from behind the splintering shutters of the bedrooms. But now the drivers were drinking beer with the bar girls and, over the radio, the Head of State was barking the first of his evening monologues.

The smallest bar girl gasped and bared her armpit in astonishment as Uncle Procopio bowed, clicked his heels and said, 'Mamzelle, I need a green chartreuse.' She fixed her eyes on his incredible moustache, poured from the bottle as if by instinct, and held her gaze till he had downed the glass and gone.

All the young Marxists came out and ogled the Mercedes as it passed.

The Da Silvas finally reached the Fort and laid the wreath.

They inspected the Independence Memorial – the last Portuguese Resident's burned-out Citroën set up on a concrete plinth.

They looked out over the south bastion at the grey lagoon, at the mangroves and the line of surf beyond.

The flourish of Arab calligraphy was a canoeman punting home.

Soft lights were seen moving along the track to the beach, up which Dom Francisco had come, down which the word 'Voodoo' made its way to the Americas.

Then they went back to Simbodji.

15

THE ANCESTRAL HOME of the Da Silvas was a mud-walled compound to the west of the taxi park, where, for a week before the Mass, the noises of rasping, thumping, grinding and sizzling had drowned the infernal chatter of weaver birds as Dom Francisco's descendants cooked the dishes he loved to eat.

Girls came back from market with pitchers of pigs' blood. Boys rode bicycles with strings of offal slung from their shoulders. Fishermen brought baskets of oysters and blue-clawed crabs. Old men brought leaves from the forest. Old women crystallized eggs in honey.

The six-year-old Grégoire da Silva pointed to a column of ants marching into an unplugged refrigerator and said, 'The refrigerator exists.'

Modeste and Pierre spent the week sloshing apricot limewash over the walls of Dom Francisco's private quarters – two long low buildings set at right-angles around the main courtyard.

Both boys stripped to the waist but wore dunces' caps of newspaper to stop the paint from caking in their hair.

They picked out the crosses over the lintels and took infinite care to mix the colour of the doors and shutters, a colour that was neither black nor purple nor brown but was the colour of themselves.

Then they set to work on the old gaming saloon.

They emptied the dead flies from a Japanese porcelain bowl. They mended a broken spittoon and nailed a hardboard sheet over the collapsed wicker seat of a sofa. They

16

scrutinized the ruins of a billiard table, without being able to imagine how one played, and flicked an ostrich feather over the frames of the pictures – for the room was also a portrait gallery.

Around the blue-washed walls hung the heads of the Da Silvas, from the Founder to the present Chief.

Dom Francisco's knotted brow and scarlet skull-cap glowered from a canvas of treacly impasto, done twenty years after his death by a wandering Sicilian artist who got stuck in Ouidah in the 1870s and had obviously earned his living from ikons of Garibaldi.

A far more competent likeness was that of his son, Isidoro da Silva, the Second Chief, painted in Bahia to celebrate his twenty-first birthday in 1837. The young mulatto dandy was shown standing in a book-lined library, wearing a blue frock-coat, a velvet cravat, and with a flowered white satin waistcoat shining over his paunch. One hand clutched at his lapel, the other fingered the diamond knop of his cane.

The portraits of his brothers, Lino and Antonio, were also the work of the Sicilian dauber. There was a sepia photograph of Cândido, the Fifth Chief, in the uniform of an Honorary Colonel of the Portuguese Infantry. And lastly there was a framed page of the souvenir catalogue of the Paris Exhibition of 1900, where Estevão da Silva and his son Agostinho-Ezekiel were exhibited as 'Fils et Petit-Fils du Négrier'.

Dom Francisco himself lay sleeping under his bed, in a chamber that overlooked a garden of red earth and plastic flowers where lizards sunned themselves on the flat white marble tombs. The room was the preserve of Yaya Adelina, a laundrywoman, who would allow no one to enter without permission.

The bed was a Goanese four-poster with ebony uprights and a headboard set with ivory medallions. But the most arresting feature was a painted plaster statue of St Francis of Assisi, his brown cassock girdled with a rope of real knots, gazing at the mildewed sheets of his namesake and lifting his hands in prayer.

A white marble plaque, set into the floor, read:

FRANCISCO MANOEL DA SILVA
Nascido em 1785 Brazil
Fālecido a 8 de março 1857 em Ajuda (Ouidah)

A wreath of arums bore the legend 'Pour Notre Illustre Aïeul!' and on a shelf stood a gilt crucifix, a yellowing Ecce Homo and a silver elephant, which was the family emblem.

Yaya Adelina carried her veneration of the ancestor to such lengths that she kept a bottle of Gordon's Gin open on the bed-table in case he should wake up.

Every morning, in case he wanted to wash, she refilled the silver water-jug cast from Maria Theresa thalers that melted when a British shell fired a warehouse in the 1840s.

From time to time she would remove the white cloth covering a rusty iron object resembling an umbrella, clotted with blood and feathers, and stuck into the floor.

This was an *Asin*, the Dahomean Altar of the Dead.

Two DAYS BEFORE the celebration there was a moment of alarm when Lieutenant-Colonel Zossoungbo Patrice of

18

the Sûreté Nationale burst in on Papa Agostinho's siesta and banned the celebration.

The colonel was twenty-four, and had long curly eye-lashes and knife-edge creases to his green paratrooper fatigues. Two grenades, the shape of scent-bottles, were slung from his belt.

Papa Agostinho wrapped a towel round his tummy and rocked his rocking chair, while the young revolu-tionary paced up and down, waving a North Korean sub-machine gun to emphasize important points:

Family festivals, he shouted, were the barbarous and fetishistic survivals of the colonial period . . .

But the afternoon was hot and the colonel was tired.

His voice rose to a childish treble. He was terrified of not making the right impression and, when Papa Agostinho made a very modest cash offer, was so re-lieved and grateful that he allowed the Da Silvas to go ahead – on one condition (he had to make a condition): they must listen to the Presidential broadcast at eight o'clock.

Then, with a smile of radiant innocence, he doffed his cap as if it were a schoolboy cap, and edged out back-wards.

His boot crushed a begonia as he went.

The colonel's visit explained the brown plastic radio blaring martial music as the guests came in to dinner.

There was a table covered with red-chequered oilcloth. Kerosene lamps spread streams of yellow light over the aerial roots of the banyan. Two mango trees, glimmering with fireflies, cut arcs of blacker velvet in the sky.

NEVER, NOT EVEN in the time of Dom Francisco, had Ouidah witnessed so unctuous a feast

Pigs' heads were anointed with gumbos and ginger. Black beans were frosted with cassava flour. Silver fish glittered in a sauce of malaguetta pepper. There was a ragout of guinea-fowl and seri-flowers, which were reputed to have aphrodisiac properties. There were mounds of fried cockscombs, salads of carrot and papaya, and pastes of shrimp, cashew nuts and coco-flesh.

The names of Brazilian dishes were on everyone's lips: *xinxin de galinha, vatapà, sarapatel, muqueca, molocoto*. There were phallic sweetmeats of tamarind and tapioca, ambrosias, bolos, babas and piles of golden patisseries.

Yaya Adelina, her head shaved and her cottons whirling with the rings of Saturn, lumbered round the table, scooping up a sample of each dish into a calabash carved with totemic animals.

Uncle Procopio moved towards the *petits-pains au chocolat* murmuring, '*Byzance!*' He had all but thrust one through his moustachios when Adelina slapped his back:

'Shame on you, sir! Eating before the Father eats!'

She set the calabash on a table outside Dom Francisco's bedroom window and covered it with a cloth of broderie anglaise.

Everyone waited for something to happen.

A GONG CLANGED. A drum rolled. Grégoire da Silva hurtled from the shadows shouting, 'Dom Francisco! Dom Francisco!' and a differently dressed procession filed into the yard.

Men in white loincloths came in with images wrapped in red stuff. Others carried chickens and a pot-bellied goat. Everyone was chanting the Founder's song: 'The Elephant spreads his net on land and sea . . . ' Their bodies were smeared with white powder and their cicatrices stood up like lumps of candlegrease.

Three young drummers were calling the Ancestor back to Earth. The sweat stuck their shirts to their skin and dark patches spread from their armpits like ink on blotting-paper.

Papa Agostinho wore coral chokers and an opera hat sequined with butterflies and a bleeding heart. His son, Africo da Silva, had on a yellow petalled crinoline, while Yaya Felicidade, in a headscarf of purple pansies, waved about a nineteenth-century English naval cutlass.

The drumbeats took the women and propelled them into the juddering movements of the dance. An effeminate in pink satin pants groaned, swayed and fell rigid as a plank.

Other women knelt before the window kneading the hamstrung goat and bellowing, 'Za! Za! Zanku! It is Night! Night!' Chickens squawked and fell silent. The knife fell on the goat's neck and its life gurgled away.

The shutters burst open to reveal Papa Agostinho

21

standing inside his grandfather's bedroom. The women handed him the foaming red calabash. He sprinkled food and blood and feathers and Gordon's Gin over the bed, the grave and Altar of the Dead.

Africo called out, 'The Dead has eaten now!' Someone predicted that rain would water the maize, and from the far end of the courtyard could be heard the booming voice of Father Olimpío: *'Syncrétisme!'*

Mrs Rosemary da Silva shook her fist and shouted, 'Ah no go fo com heah fo no juju!' and stamped off, followed by her husband.

Everyone agreed the Nigerians had no manners.

While the votaries dressed and changed, the band relaxed into a Brazilian samba. Father Olimpío took his place at the head of the table:

'Bénissez-nous, Mon Dieu, pour la nourriture que nous mangeons ce soir . . .'

THROUGHOUT DINNER, THE President's voice came in cracked bursts: there was something the matter with the radio. He called on the People to break the 'umbilical cord of International Imperialism' and, when lost for words, would howl, 'Down with Intellectuals!' or 'Death to Mercenaries and the Lackeys of Capitalism!'

Nobody took much notice.

Stuffing his face with cornpaste, Hermengildo da Silva made no secret of the fact that he had sacrificed a goat to Gu, the God of War. Mama Benz hiccoughed. Adelina sneezed and sprayed pineapple juice over the table. Uncle Procopio offered to play Dvořák's *Humoresque*; and

22

the twin brothers, Euclides and Policarpo, squabbled about whether the family motto should read, 'Flies are not visible in society!' or 'Flies are not acceptable in society!'

But as usual, the favourite topic was the loss of Dom Francisco's fortune; and as usual, the family's 'German', Karl-Heinrich (Gazozo) da Silva, set his fists on the table and began his annual dissertation:

'I have it on the authority of my late father, Anton Wilhelm, that Our Illustrious Ancestor deposited thirty-six million U.S. dollars in a Swiss bank . . . '

'It wasn't a Swiss bank,' Agostinho interrupted. 'It was the Banco Coutinho in Bahia.'

'Petrification,' shrieked the President, ' . . . Paralysation! . . . Mystification! . . . Mummification!'

'And that your Uncle Antonio . . . '

'They weren't dollars. They were cruzeiros . . . '

' . . . lost the paper . . . '

'He didn't lose it. He drank it.'

' . . . to sensibilize . . . to organize . . . to mobilize . . . '

'I tell you, he burned the paper from the bank. He put it in a glass. Then he poured in a bottle of champagne and drank the lot.'

'I don't believe you.'

'It was a big glass.'

'And the fleet?' asked Yaya Adelina. 'What happened to the fleet?'

'Sunk by the British.'

' . . . to defeat this macabre plot to massacre our people . . . '

'Stolen by the Brazilian Government.'

'They should give it back.'

'They won't give it back.'

'We should start a process.'

' . . . to steal the incredible riches of our country . . . '

'Peanuts,' said Uncle Procopio.

'Peanuts?'

'We'd starve without peanuts.'

' . . . and the thunderous riposte of our Armed Forces . . . '

'And palm-oil . . . '

' . . . and our scientific and operational regime . . . '

'But peanuts give you cancer.'

'But they're all we've got.'

Africo da Silva said the President was giving him a headache. Gustave said you got headaches from the harmattan. Someone else said you got them from fruit bats, and Papa Agostinho wound up wearily by saying that Dom Francisco was ruined the year the United States stopped using cowrie-shells for money.

Mama Benz asked what a cowrie really was.

'Cowrie is a snail,' he said. 'It lives in a river called Mississippi. In the old days, the Americans would throw a slave in the river, the cowries would feed on the body, and then they'd haul it up and that's how they got money to buy more slaves.'

'Revolution or Death!'

'So when they passed the law, there were no more cowries . . . '

'Marxist-Leninism is our only philosophical guide!'

' . . . and that's how Dom Francisco was ruined!'

'Ah! Cette chinoiserie de la Révolution!' Gustave da Silva shook his lovely head.

'And the fleet?' wailed Yaya Adelina. 'Whatever became of the fleet?'

TWO

AT TWENTY-FIVE minutes past eight, a woman's wail rose up from the belly of the compound.

'Ey . . . yeo . . . yo . . . yo . . . o . . . o . . . o . . . wo . . . wo . . . wo . . . !'

The diners widened their arms and went silent. A girl, all arms and legs, rushed in.

'It's Mama Wéwé,' she shouted. 'She won't eat.'

Shooing Muscovy ducks before them, the Da Silvas followed the girl down an alley to the house with purple shutters.

They peered in. Moths whirled around a glutinous patch of lamplight.

Dom Francisco's own daughter, Wéwé the White One, the proof that he was white, lay dying at the far end of the room.

Mademoiselle Eugenia da Silva, a skeleton who happened to breathe, lay dying on an etruscan couch of jacaranda wood carved with anacardiums and passion flowers. Beside her was a plate of shredded papaya, un-eaten.

Her tongue had locked to the roof of her mouth. Her lips had sunk without trace into the crevasses of her chin. Only her nose was visible, rearing from the tatters of a black lace bonnet, and the great white hands lying be-tween the bones of her pelvis in a hollow of black bom-bazine.

The Da Silvas gazed at the miracle. That she should continue to live was not incredible. She was not that

27

much older than Sagbadjou the King, who lived with his wives and retainers in a bungalow behind the palace at Abomey.

That she should die was unthinkable.

Sometimes, on cooler evenings, her shutter would creak open. The boys playing naked in the yard would cluster round and a withered white arm would reach through the close black curtains and feel for their heads.

Sometimes they saw her face, the skin transparent as a gecko's and the green eyes milky with cataracts.

She still had power in her fingers. They would skim over the tight curls, but if they touched a head of straight hair, they would stroke and caress it, and the second hand would pass through the curtains and reward its owner with a coin of Louis Napoleon or Queen Victoria.

She lived *en princesse*, they said, on a diet of bean paste and papaya, drinking a little mango juice or an infusion of citronella grass. Her only companion was a withered crone called Mãe Roxa, who prepared and tasted her food: Mama Wéwé was still terribly afraid of being poisoned.

In 1953, at the celebrations of her hundredth birthday, she had pointed a finger at her relatives and said, 'Remember you are Brazilians!' She had never spoken since. The years went by without her ever opening her mouth except for food.

Before she withdrew into silence, Papa Agostinho was the one man whose presence she would tolerate. He would listen as she rambled over the disordered events of the century: of Amazons drumming in the courtyard; of the arms of General Dodds, 'quite hairy for a mulatto', or 'that animal' by which she meant Mère Agathe of the Petites Soeurs des Pauvres.

28

But when Agostinho asked her about the existence of some lost papers and tried to steer the conversation to the events of March 1857, she curled her lip.

EXACTLY NINETY-EIGHT years ago she fell in love.

She was tall and beautiful. Her skin was golden and her black hair streaked with auburn. She had eyes of greenish amber, the colour of a troubled sea. The corners of her mouth lifted in a perpetual smile from pronouncing the slushed, suggestive consonants of Brazilian Portuguese. At the sight of her swaying walk men had to hold themselves – yet, at the time, she was a virgin.

One evening, when the harmattan was blowing, she met the English agent coming up from the beach. He told her of a merchantman at anchor in the roads. On board was a professor who had come to collect the plants and animals of Dahomey.

That night she lay awake and tried to picture the professor. At sunrise she put on a dress of white muslin embroidered with blue flowers. She tied a ribbon to her straw hat and went with Mr Townsend to the shore.

Crabs scuttled sideways as they trod down the scarp of white sand. Through the mist they saw the hull and rolling yardarms: as it cleared they saw the red of her ensign and black dots which were the passengers and crew.

But the surf was running high. No passengers could land and the krumen went back to their huts.

Five days later the sea was down. Mr Townsend signalled the 'All Clear!' She watched the canoe prows rear through the foam, and the backs of the krumen in a fitful sun.

Sharks swam between the inner and outer line of breakers, waiting for a capsize: they were said to have a taste for white flesh. The fetish-man stood in the shallows rattling a chaplet as the first canoe came in. She prayed as well. She could hardly bear to watch the men paddling as they tried to keep it straight.

The canoe roared over a crest and thudded on the shingle: black arms whisked the passengers ashore before the next wave broke.

The professor shook hands with Mr Townsend, rubbed the salt from his spectacles and began checking his pile of equipment. He was a heavy man, purple in the face, wearing a jacket with a lot of pockets and a pith-helmet and a veil.

In the first rush of her disappointment, she did not take in the tall, freckle-faced lieutenant with his red moustache and blue eyes the colour of the market-women's beads – and then she understood the pounding of her heart.

That evening he came to Simbodji with a request for hammockeers: he was going to Abomey with a message to deliver to the King.

At dinner he wore the blue and gold mess uniform of the Queen's 2nd West India Regiment, which was stationed at Cape Coast Castle. She spoke a little English and he said, 'We'll soon put a stop to that pidgin.'

Slowly, so she should understand every word, he told her of the Queen of England and the City of London. She tried to imagine snow – soft and white like the down of the silk-cotton tree, but cold, how cold she could not guess.

She played the Swiss musical boxes that had once belonged to her father. They watched the steel combs and the bristling brass cylinders that turned erratically because the combs were corroded with rust. He tried to sing Schubert's 'Trout', but the tempo was far too erratic and they ended up laughing.

Then she found the key to the box that played waltzes. Not knowing the steps, she let her feet drift and the weight of her body fall on his hand in the small of her back.

He played billiards with her half-brother Antonio and allowed him to win. She heard them murmuring in English and, when she looked in their direction, saw the avid blue eyes through clouds of Havana smoke.

Next morning he came with presents: two scarves of Madras silk, a marcasite necklace and a gilt toilet mirror – all intended for the ladies of the King.

At sunset they walked to the garden at Zomai where Dom Francisco had built a Chinese pavilion. The trunks of the mango trees had been whitewashed and the breeze stirred a glissando of coco fronds.

The pavilion had upturned eaves and round windows that were no longer round. The old gardener had swept it clean as if for a picnic. He slipped away as they came in and she thought, 'So my brother arranged all this.'

Her forelip tingled from the bristles of his moustache. His hands were gentle at first but she could feel them hardening. Her dress ripped as she tore herself away.

He dropped her in surprise. She did not scream. She ran from the garden into the red street, where some Fon drummer boys were practising. They jeered and thumbed her and struck up a thumping rhythm as she passed.

31

She shut herself in her room and lay face downward on the brass bed covered with country cloths. Only when her pillow was wet through did she realize the extent of her loneliness.

Not that she had been ignorant of what to expect. Virgins were broken at Simbodji with the ease of bursting seed pods. From childhood she had known the coarse laughter of women as they sniffed the bloodstained rag. Her half-brothers had tried to force her. Her half-sisters pursed their lips if approached by anyone darker than themselves – yet they were always willing to whore to white sailors.

An unlearned code of honour had stopped her sinking to their level.

But when he came back in the morning, mumbling apologies, she fell, a lovely automaton, into his arms.

She said, 'Take me with you!'

'I will,' he said, and instantly regretted it.

THE PORTERS WERE ready to carry the expedition up-country.

The lieutenant and the professor lay on the blue-and-white striped hammocks. The porters lifted their weight as if it were nothing, and they set off with a clatter of gongs and retching of ivory trumpets. The last she saw of them was a khaki sleeve waving as they went out of sight.

For three weeks her mood varied from euphoria to despair. Then, late one night, a boy ran over from Mr

Townsend's house: the younger white had come back sick, very sick; and the professor had been kept by the King.

The colour of his face had gone beyond the white of the bed-curtains. His eyes were yellow and his mouth was grey, foaming at the edges, babbling names that meant nothing to her. Mr Townsend diagnosed an attack of malaria that would, perhaps, be fatal. He had run out of quinine, but had the sense not to despise the remedy she fetched from the herbalist. He rammed it down the throat of the patient, who recovered.

As the fever left him, he would shout hysterically, 'Get me out of here! Do something!' and when Mr Townsend told him of a Dutch brig at anchor, he said, 'Get me aboard!'

None of the King's subjects was allowed to leave Dahomey without permission, so she had to go down to the beach under guard. His manner was correct but his voice was cold: from England he would send the passage money, and the bride-price.

It was a grey and windless day but the crashing breakers wafted a current of air that set her muslin dress flapping between her legs. She waved a scarf as the canoe shoved off. He did not wave back but stared out to sea, fixedly, at the waiting ship.

She waited six months, a year, two years. She learned the art of lace-making from a slavewoman freed from Bahia. Together they made headcloths, petticoats and napkins: she was anxious to possess every accomplishment.

She taught herself to read. She pretended to read, but though she could distinguish one page from another, though she could even memorize the letters on a page, she was never able to unravel the sense from the lines.

Hoping to master more English, she went each Thursday to the service of hymn-singing in the Methodist Chapel. The Reverend Bernabo was a Sierra Leone mulatto, who had Dundreary whiskers and had been educated in England. He taught her the scales on a tinny upright piano and soon, to the toc-toc of the metronome, she was playing 'Abide with Me!' or 'Mine Eyes have seen the Glory of the Coming of the Lord!'

The missionary's daughters adored her. They would all wear white together and, when they sang, a wide-eyed crowd was sure to gather at the gate. She was bitterly upset to learn they hired themselves to pay for their father's drink.

She went on long walks alone.

On thundery afternoons, when perpendicular clouds towered high in the sky, she would wander through the palm-groves to the lagoon and watch the black-and-white kingfishers flutter over the dark water.

Sometimes she walked inland to the campsites of the Peuls. These were a light-skinned people who slept under the stars and kept their beauty into old age. The harmattan brought them down from the savannah to the coast. Their lyre-horned cattle moved through the grass with a crackling sound. She welcomed their coming: the dry season also brought Europeans to the shore.

Her eyes would question Mr Townsend but pride prevented her from asking for news. He tried to avoid her: the callousness of his countryman embarrassed him. Only when his company recalled him did he find the courage to tell her of the professor's letter: the lieutenant had resigned his commission, married and settled in Somerset.

'Oh!' she said.

He had expected an outburst of grief and held out a hand to comfort her. But she stared at him as if he were mad and ran off, singing and dancing barefoot in the sand, to where some krumen were landing empty palm-oil puncheons from a ship.

THE YEARS HARDENED the contours of her face into angular planes. A pinched look came into the corners of her eyes. Her skin stretched tight over her nose and cheekbones, and fell in loose folds down her throat. At thirty she was an old maid, but after that her appearance hardly changed: the Slave Coast takes its victims young or pickles them to great antiquity.

One by one, her acquaintance narrowed to her maid, her Mahi slave-boy, her father and the red-haired stranger. Unable to make the distinction between the real and the supernatural, she made none between the living, the absent and the dead.

For all she cared, her relatives were the masks of a nightmare. And in their turn, the Da Silvas looked on the white childless woman with superstitious awe.

They suspected her of the Evil Eye. They took care to burn their loose hair and nail clippings. The women said she prowled round Simbodji at night, scooping up earth impregnated with their spittle.

Since no one would sleep under the same roof, they left her in possession of Joaquim da Silva's old villa at the far end of the compound. She bought a bolt of black cloth and draped it round her room. She took to wearing black herself, a stiff dress reaching to her calves and a lace bonnet tied under her chin.

For years she had lavished affection on her father's macaw, a bad-tempered bird called Zé Piranha, which pecked at strangers and its own feathers till it died of inanition. She then transferred her love to a scabby bitch with mastitis that lay all day in the shade of a banana, but at sunset would sit by the steps and howl.

Simbodji decayed. The roofs collapsed and the walls crumbled. Livid weeds smothered the piles of rubble, which were left to lizards, scorpions and snakes. Deprived of their revenues from the Slave Trade, the Da Silvas sank into tropical torpor.

In 1882 a tornado hit Dom Francisco's house, whirled its pantiles in the air and scattered them over the town.

In 1884 a girl was grilling cashew nuts when one burst from her brazier and set a roof on fire. Thirteen houses burned to the ground.

In 1887 Cândido da Silva, one of Dom Francisco's youngest sons, was elected Head of the Family on the strength of his talent for repairing the fortune. He even got the King of Dahomey to put his cross to a document that turned Ouidah over to the Portuguese as a protectorate.

The colonizers came with a military band from the island of São Tomé, and staked out the site for a barracks. The King sent Cândido a flattering message inviting him up to Abomey. And he left, in his Portuguese Colonel's uniform, with his wives, children, umbrella-bearers, musicians and an Amazon guard of honour.

He did not come back.

The Portuguese major, who went to ask for his comrade-in-arms, was shown into a mud house with a pair of executioners' knives flanking the doorway. The honorary colonel sat trussed to a European chair, still in his epaulettes, with an iron chain round his neck and a wooden gag shoved down his throat. At his feet was a silver bowl, buzzing with flies.

'Into that bowl', the officer was told, 'go the heads of all who trouble the Kingdom.'

Nine days later, a detachment of Amazons burst into Simbodji in uniforms sewn with the crocodile insignia of their brigade.

They fired their muskets in the air and danced the decapitation dance, warning the Da Silvas that if they dared sell one grain of Dahomean soil, the house would be broken, razed, obliterated; and they would be sent to work the Royal Plantations, or to tell the King's ancestors how things stood in this perfidious world.

For months Simbodji was wrapped in the silence of the tomb.

SENHORINHA EUGENIA TOOK advantage of the catastrophe to carry off some of Dom Francisco's relics, as if, by collecting his possessions, she could restore him to life.

She took his silver-mounted cigar case; his pink opaline chamber pot; his ivory-handled slave-brand with the initials F.S.; his rosary of carnauba nuts; some scraps of paper covered with his handwriting; a lithograph of the Emperor Dom Pedro II; a picture of a Brazilian house, and a particularly bloodthirsty canvas of Judith hacking off the head of Holophernes.

37

Her fellow-raider on these expeditions was Cândido da Silva's ten-year-old son, Cesário. He had got left behind when his parents went up to Abomey, and was now an orphan.

With his green eyes and wad of blond hair, Cesário was a throwback to an earlier strain in the family. And as young birds will expel an albino from their nest, the other boys made his life a misery and pelted him with filth and rotten fruit.

The climate disagreed with him. The sun peeled his skin leaving pink patches. There was a permanent scab on the bridge of his nose, and his mosquito bites would come up in welts and go septic.

He came to her one morning with chiggers in his left foot.

She laid him down, sharpened a knife blade, cut through the leathery sole, and scoured out the sack of eggs. He didn't even whimper. She kissed him on the forehead and took him to live with her.

She had never looked after a child and each day brought something new. She recovered her lilting walk and dazzling smile. The colour returned to her face. She threw off her black, put hoops of gold in her ears, and strode through the market in a dress of bright flowers.

She dressed Cesário in long whites, made him wear a panama of palm fibre and, in this uniform, sent him to the French Fathers to learn how to read. He would come home with stories of railways and knights-in-armour and all kinds of useful information: the Ancestors were, in fact, Gauls; the cows of Haute-Savoie gave six times more milk than cows in Africa.

He particularly liked the story of Moses and Pharaoh and kept asking whether Pharaoh was the same as the

King of Dahomey: he was unimpressed when told he was not.

On rainy days she would take out a colour print distributed by the Church Missionary Society in Abeokuta, and she would point to the greybeard beckoning the traveller up the 'Straight and Narrow Path' and say, 'Look! It's a picture of your grandfather!'

Or they would spread out a panorama of Bahia and he would read off the names: 'Casa Santa da Misericórdia . . . Monastery of São Bento . . . Convent of Santa Teresa . . .' while her eyes ranged over the domes, towers and pediments which reminded her of the New Jerusalem floating down from Heaven.

She tried to picture the house they would live in when they went back to the City. She spoke of dancing in Bahia, in a tall blue room lined with mirrors and pillars of gold – which was quite untrue, for she had never strayed further than Ouidah.

At other times they would call on the Germans. In 1890 a Hamburg trading company called Goedelt bought the concession of the old British Fort. The newcomers drank beer from stoneware tankards and, in the evening, their mess-room clouded over with pipe-smoke. A cuckoo clock, painted with red roses, hung on the wall and there were pictures of the Rhinemaidens and one of the young Kaiser Wilhelm II.

Cesário was the favourite of Herr Raabe the director, who thought of training him as a book-keeper. Whenever Eugenia went over to fetch him, she brought a chicken or some fruit and would stand on one foot, shyly, in the doorway, rubbing her calf with the other foot and staring at the wall.

The Germans thought she was waiting for the cuckoo.

When the bird popped out of its hutch, they would say in English, 'That's enough now, old lady. Thank you. Time to go home!' and when the door shut, in German, 'My god, how that woman stares!'

But she had only been staring at the Kaiser.

ONE EVENING SHE and Cesário were crossing the Sogbadji Quarter in the stillness that precedes a storm. White flags hung motionless over a fetish. Some old men were crouching in the shadows, whitewashed all over, with their heads hung low. Unusual numbers of turkey-buzzards were converging on the town.

From one house they heard a low moan; from another mourners carried a corpse wrapped in a reed mat with the feet poking out. They saw a man dragging himself into the bushes. There were patches of vomit and yellow excrement all down the street.

The cholera had come ashore with the crew of a ship.

They hurried home. She bolted the door and would admit no one: she knew that much about contagion.

At dusk on the third day, Cesário felt dizzy and had to lie down. Within an hour he had fouled his bed. Sweat streamed from his skin leaving it cold, inelastic and clammy. His eyes sank in their sockets and gaped, expressionless, at the rafters. He did not lose consciousness and locked his shrivelled fingers tightly round hers.

The crisis came at that moment in an African dawn when everything is golden. Doves were cooing in the

40

garden. A shaft of sunlight fell through the window and framed the woman in blue who kneeled by the boy's bed. Cramps racked his body and his ribcage writhed like a concertina.

She bent over and kissed him, slowly sliding her tongue into his dry mouth, praying for the disease to leave him and come to her.

He gasped, 'Do leave me alone,' and soon he left her.

She went on living.

She went to a Brazilian trader and bought a length of azure cloth, the colour the Angels wore in Heaven. She washed the body, which had already taken on a greenish tinge. She wrapped it and laid it in a coffin of iroko wood. She fluffed his hair round like a halo. She put a gold coin in his hand and her gardener nailed down the lid.

They buried him in the family cemetery, under Dom Francisco's window, with a cross of palm-fronds set over his head. None of her relations took any notice, being too distracted by their own deaths.

Three days later, Raabe's assistant saw her walking on the beach, her chin pressed against her throat, muttering and watching the sand squeeze between her toes.

Then she laughed and held her hands wide and waved a black scarf at the birdless sea.

He asked what she was doing and she said, 'He's gone to Bahia.'

THE NEXT FEW years washed over her without disturbing her solitude.

She failed to notice the outburst of human sacrifice that

41

marked the accession of the new King, Behanzin the 'Shark'. She ignored the French bombardment of Ouidah which killed a hundred and thirty people and dismembered a sacred baobab. Nor did she celebrate when Estevão da Silva hauled an improvised tricolour up the flagpole and started the family on their career as brown Frenchmen.

The events of her life were the palm-nut harvest and the festivals of the Brazilian Church. For three weeks before Saints Cosmas and Damian in September, she and her maid, Roxa, would sew frilly dresses for the twin sisters of the town, who were almost worshipped as divinities. In January, they would help paint the mummers' costumes for the Bumba-Meu-Boi. And every 3rd of June, on John the Baptist's Day, they sat outside the chapel of the Portuguese Fort grilling ears of new corn for the congregants.

Because these occasions repeated themselves year after year, she lost all sense of growing old.

Mãe Roxa died in the smallpox epidemic of 1905 after refusing an inoculation. Her place was taken by an eighteen-year-old 'Brazilian' girl, whose real name was Cristella Chaves, but Eugenia would make no concession to the change, called her Roxa and expected her to know all about the last fifty years.

By 1914 the Chapel of the Fort had fallen into decay. She had long coveted the image of the Baptist's head and, to preserve it from looters, she took it away for safe-keeping. The head had glass eyes and snaky black curls and was the work of an African sculptor in Bahia who had carved the aorta, the oesophagus and third neck vertebra with meticulous attention to detail. He had screwed it to a Minton meat-dish stencilled with mauve carnations:

42

painted blood trickled into the scoop intended to catch juices from the roast beef of Old England.

Her next idea was to convert Dom Francisco's bedroom into a shrine.

She and Roxa made rosaries. They made reliquaries. They made wreaths of artificial flowers from sea-shells and they improvised a Holy Ghost from a Pirevitte teapot in the form of a chicken. They hung up the panorama of Bahia, the picture of Judith and some religious colour prints: Santa Marta with a pair of bleeding hearts; Santa Luzia smiling at her own two eyes lying in the palm of her hand.

The head of the Baptist they set on the altar table.

Then, with the work all but finished, she hit on the idea of buying a statue of St Francis to stand at the foot of her father's bed.

The palm-nut buyer, Monsieur Poidevineau, advanced some money on her share of the crop and sent off to Marseille to a company that specialized in sacred sculpture.

The Poverello arrived at the railway station in a stout box. The Brazil-town band beat out a samba and Mama Wéwé – as she was now called – stood smiling on the platform as the train drew in. For the first time in twenty-five years she was not wearing black.

The Fathers of Our Lady of Africa heard of this touching example of faith and offered their help. But she would allow no one in the shrine until she was ready for the consecration.

One morning Fathers Truitard, Boët and Zérringer walked down to Simbodji in spotless white soutanes and sandals. She unbolted the door and ushered them in with a gesture of triumph.

43

They saw the head of Holophernes, the head of the Baptist, the slave chains, a toilet mirror and the nails and bloodstained feathers. Father Zérringer, who was an amateur zoologist, looked over the reliquaries and identified a vulture's claw, a python vertebra, a fragment of baboon skull and the eardrum of a lion.

'*Ce sont les gri-gris du marché,*' he whispered.

Knowing him to be less liable to sectarian anger, Father Truitard's colleagues deputed him to tell her the truth. He was an embarrassed man, with a pitted face and kind brown eyes, who had spent years communing with waves and petrels on the island of Ushant. He knew some Portuguese.

Mother Church, he explained, could not allow the worship of idolatrous objects on Holy Ground. The Faith was there. The heart was willing and the Flesh was willing. But she did need some lessons in scripture. Nor was the choice of St Francis a wise one to stand over the grave of a slaver.

'But he sent them to PARADISE!' she screamed, and pointed to the panorama of Bahia.

'But St Francis, my sister, was a poor wanderer, who loved all men and the birds and the animals . . . '

She was not listening. A hoarse cry tore from her lips. Her arms lashed out and flapped helplessly. She hurled herself out into the blazing sun and fell down in a heap.

Two days later, Mère Agathe of the Petites Soeurs des Pauvres barged past Roxa and forced her way into Eugenia's room. She withdrew after five minutes, her face scratched to ribbons and her habit a massacre of carmine.

MAMA WÉWÉ SAT another sixty years in the curdled odour of rotting brocade, her eyes glued to her father's portable oratory of the Last Supper.

This was a glass-fronted vitrine, the size of a small doll's house and made by the nuns of the Soledade in Bahia:

The miniature room had sky-blue walls, mirrors and gilded pilasters. On the floor there was a marquetry sunburst and, under a glass dome on the mantelpiece, a clock. Wooden figures of Christ and the Apostles were sitting down to a meal of plaster-of-Paris chicken. The eyes of Our Lord were the colour of turquoise and his head bristled with real red hair. In her imagination she would contract her body and stand watching in the door-way – though she would step aside for the shifty mulatto who left in the middle of the dinner.

The years slipped by and nobody repaired the house. The thatch rotted, the shutters splintered and, when ants undermined the floor, her rocking chair would no longer rock. Weeds sprang up in the rainy season, bleached for lack of light. Patches of mould spread over the walls: a delta of red streams fanned out from the wasps' nests in the rafters and cut across the termite trails.

Only once, in 1942, was there a break in the rhythm of her days.

After a noisy *vin d'honneur*, the Resident's wife, Madame Burlaton, mistook the accelerator for the brake of her Peugeot and distributed Aizan, the Market Fetish, in pieces all over the square. The *féticheurs* demanded a

45

human sacrifice for the reconsecration. Her husband refused. There was a riot.

A platoon of Senegalese spahis fired, killing a goat and wounding a woman in the leg. Roxa heard the shots and, four hours later, ran to the barracks with a message for their commanding officer: Mademoiselle da Silva would be delighted to receive him.

Lieutenant André Parisot had heard of the mysterious white woman whom nobody had seen. He took some time to macassar his hair and put on his best whites.

'Lieutenant,' she said. 'I shall play to celebrate your victory. Roxa, fetch me my piano!'

Roxa carried in a white plank painted with thirty-five black keys, and the lieutenant chewed his lip as her uncut fingernails scratched the arpeggios and dust fell out of the wormholes.

Dom Francisco's wardrobe, held together by its paint surface alone, lasted until 1957, when it collapsed, revealing a wreckage of whalebone stays and shreds of black taffeta that fluttered upwards like flakes of carbonized paper.

Spiders had turned the parrot cage into a grey tent. The pictures were peeling, and all Twelve Apostles eaten away to leprous stumps.

Yet, from the head of Christ, like the periscopic eyes of certain fish, two blue glass beads stood out on stalks.

HER OWN EYES were too tired to see the faces peering in at the window. But she had seen the same faces long ago, and they were all there, as she imagined.

46

Unscrewing a silver phial, Father Olimpío da Silva gave extreme unction and the room resounded with his prayer. Modeste swung a censer and the clouds of blue smoke disturbed the wasps and set them buzzing.

She was not sweating. Her face was still. No one would have thought that, under that papery skin, there were veins and arteries and a pumping heart.

Then her lips opened with an audible pop. The Da Silvas heard a rustling sound. At first, they were uncertain if it were the rustle of her skin, the rustle of black bombazine, or the start of the death rattle.

A word detached itself and floated around the room. A second word came clear. A string of words, faint as the wind in distant palms.

'The papers,' they whispered. 'Ask her about the papers.'

Papa Agostinho put his ear to her mouth. He got up and tiptoed to the window.

'She speaking Portuguese. Who speaks Portuguese? Doesn't anyone speak Portuguese?'

THREE

THE MAN WHO landed at Ouidah in 1812 was born, twenty-seven years earlier, near Jaicos in the Sertão, the dry scrubby cattle country of the Brazilian North-East.

The Sertanistas are wild and poor. They have tight faces, sleek hair and sometimes the green eyes of a Dutch or Celtic ancestor. They hate negroes. They believe in miraculous cures, and their legends tell of a phantom king called Dom Sebastião, who will rid the earth of Antichrist.

Like all people born in thorny places, they dream of green fields and a life of ease. Sometimes, with light hearts, they set out south for San Salvador da Bahia, but when they see the sea and the city, they panic and turn back to the badlands.

Francisco Manoel's father, a hired hand on a ranch, was killed while driving steers at a round-up. His leather hat caught in the fork of two branches: the chinstrap slipped round his neck and throttled him. Friends following the tracks of his riderless horse found the body dangling with the feet just clear of the ground.

His son was one year old.

The mother was a very bad-tempered woman. Her hands were worked raw. Blue veins stood out on her temples and her thinning hair failed to hide the wens that had sprouted in several places on her scalp. Years of drought had set her mouth in an expression of rage – rage for her shrivelled breasts; for the bast sandals instead of shoes; for the feather bed she would never

51

own, or the white metal crucifix that should have been made of gold.

She spent most days crouching in the speckled shade of an acacia, smoking a stone pipe.

The house had a grass roof and walls of packed mud and scantlings and stood in open country in a clump of umbu trees. The shutters were painted a cool blue, but the coolness was an illusion.

A barricade of bromelias fenced in the yard. Nearby, there was a cattle-tank with duckweed and, beyond that, the thornscrub, rising and falling in grey-green sweeps, punctuated here and there by black candelabra cacti.

The three rooms were bare, whitewashed, flyblown. Folded hammocks hung like hams from the rafters: the saddles, hats and halters hung in the porch. There was a statuette of Onuphrius to guard the door and one of St Blaise to keep off ants. The woman kept a white cloth on the altar table long after she had stopped praying for anything in particular.

Within weeks of her husband's death, she took up with an Indian half-breed called Manuelzinho, who came to the house one day and asked for water. He had a hare-lip and teeth like bits of rusty metal. The tie-strings of his jerkin stretched taut across his chest, and people thought they were going to snap. He killed snakes for a living and sold the flaky white flesh at market.

His horse had one ear clean off, and when they asked, 'What happened to that horse's ear?' he'd say gloomily, 'It got eaten by bugs.'

The boy's first memories were of watching the pair, creaking night and day in a sisal hammock: he never knew a time he was not a stranger.

Yet whenever the man satisfied her, the woman's voice

became less rasping and her mouth would ease into a smile. She took trouble with meals, combed her son's hair for lice, and told the old stories of Dom Sebastião and the Princess Magalona.

Remembering happier times, she told him the riddles she had learned as a child: the avocado which had the 'heart of a bull'; or the 'girls in a castle clothed in yellow', who were a bunch of bananas. And then there was his particular favourite:

> *Igrejinha bem rondinha*
> *Bem branquinha*
> *Não tem porta*
> *Não tem janela*
> *Dentro dela tem tesouros*
> *Um de prata, outro d'oro.*

– a little round white church, without a window and without a door: yet inside it had two treasures, one of silver, one of gold – to which the answer was 'Egg'.

But Manuelzinho was a born wanderer. After a week of captivity he was ready to move on. He would pace round the yard glaring at the sun as though it were setting late. Or he would flay the dust with a whip, or sit throwing knives at a log.

Then as the woman watched him dwindle to an ash-coloured speck, her fingers would claw the table top and the splinters got in under her nails.

MANY YEARS LATER, chained hand and foot in the King of Dahomey's prison, Francisco Manoel would remember the year of the drought.

That summer – he was seven at the time – the clouds banked up as usual and burst. For five days rain drenched the earth, seedlings sprouted and there were clouds of yellow butterflies everywhere. Then the clouds went away. The sun quivered in a blue metal sky. The mud cracked.

One sunset, mother and son watched the formations of duck flying south. She hugged him and said, 'The ducks are flying to the river.'

Hot winds blew, hiding the horizon in dust and blowing pellets of goat dung across the yard. When the tank dried up, the cattle stood around the patch of green slime, groaning, with their muzzles full of spines.

In a cabin behind the house lived an old Cariri Indian called Felix, who looked after the widow's few animals in return for food and a roof. One evening, he collapsed in the kitchen and, in a hoarse and hopeless voice, said, 'All of them are dying.' He had cut lengths of cactus, stripped them of spines, and set them out for fodder: but the cattle had gone on dying.

Blood flowed from their flanks from the little pink lumps that were ticks. They slashed themselves trying to reach a single unwithered leaf and, when they did die, the hides were so tough that carrion birds could not break through to the guts.

Fires tore through the country with a resinous crackling, leaving velvety stumps where once there had been trees. The flames caught Felix as he was hacking out a firebreak, and they found him, charred and sheeny, with a grimace of white teeth and green mucus running out of his nose. The woman dug a grave, but a dog unearthed the body and chewed it apart.

Rats ran down the boy's hammock strings and bit him as he slept. Rattlesnakes came into the yard, attracted by anything that still had life. When a column of driver-ants swept through the house, the woman had only the energy to save a saucepan of manioc flour and some strips of wind-dried beef.

Finally, when she had lost hope, Manuelzinho rode out of the thornscrub, where he had lived on the half-roasted bodies of rodents. He dug deeper down the well-shaft and came back with a dribble of foul ferruginous liquid. But within a week all three water jars were empty.

The boy's mouth cracked and ulcerated. His eyelids blazed. His legs went stiff. They gave him mashed palm-roots to eat but they swelled in his stomach and the cramps forced him to lie down. All the moisture seemed to have drained from his body. There was no question of being able to cry – even as his mother entered her death agony.

They woke that morning to find her left leg hanging limply over the lip of her hammock. Manuelzinho lifted the cloth that covered her face from the flies. Unspeaking, and with the terrible tenderness of people pushed to the limit, she pleaded for the son whom she had starved herself to save.

Her oases were not of this world: she died in the night without a groan.

The boy watched Manuelzinho bury her. They started south for the river. They passed knots of migrants too tired to go on. Black birds sat waiting on the branches.

The horse died on the second day, but men are tougher than horses.

They reached the river at the ferry station of Santa Maria da Boavista, where Manuelzinho left the orphan with the priest and rode away.

The boy remembered nothing of the journey, yet for years he would keep back a lump of meat and sleep with it under his pillow.

SANTA MARIA DA Boavista lay on the north bank of the São Francisco River as it sweeps in a great arc through the provinces of Bahia and Pernambuco.

It had a single street of pantiled houses strung out along a rocky ridge. Below, the muddy waters sluiced by, carrying rafts of vegetation from a greener country upstream. A white church crowned the highest point: above the scrolls of its pediment, a plain blue cross melted the sufferings of the Crucifixion into a cloudless sky.

The boy's guardian, Father Menezes Brito, was a fat conceited Portuguese, who had been exiled here for some misdemeanour: his one amusement was to baptize Indian babies with his spittle. He fed Francisco Manoel and let him sleep in a shed. Hoping to claim him for the Church, he taught him to ring a carillon of bells, the rudiments of Latin, some simple mathematics and the art of writing letters in italic script.

He told him of Bahia and its three hundred churches, of the city of Lisbon and the Holy House of Rome. He made him play the role of St Sebastian at Corpus Christi processions. He called him 'my green-eyed angel' yet made him grovel and confess the blackness of his soul. Sometimes he led him into a bedroom reeking of incense and dead flowers, where he kissed him.

The village boys called the newcomer 'Chico Diabo' and were always plotting to hurt him: he had only to glare in their faces and they shrank back.

His one friend was the black boy, Pepeu, whom he held in thrall. Together they plucked finches alive, made certain experiments with the flesh of a watermelon, and shouted obscenities at the girls washing tripes in the river.

Once, they tried crucifying a cat, but it got away.

On market days, they went down to the slaughter-house where old hags would be fighting with pariah dogs over offal. The butchers wore red caps and breeches of blue nankeen that were always purple, and they would splash about in the blood, puffing at cigars and pole-axing any animal still left standing.

The cows stared unamazed at their murderers.

'Like the Saints,' said Francisco Manoel.

He knew, far better than the priest, the meaning of Christ's martyrdom, and the liturgy of thorns and blood and nails. He knew God made men to rack them in the wilderness, yet his own sufferings had hardened him to the sufferings of others. By the age of thirteen, he wore an agate-handled knife in his belt, took pains to clip his moustache, and showed not a trace of squeamishness when he went to watch a flogging at the pillory.

Every October, as the cashews ripened in the last of the

rains, the cowhands from the outlying ranches would round up their herds and begin the long trek south to the markets of Bahia. Files of cattle converged on the town. They were cumbersome animals, with swinging dewlaps and hides the colour of cornmeal; and the men would ride around in clouds of dust yelling, 'É . . . Hou . . . Hé . . . Hé . . . O . . . O . . . O . . . O . . .!'

Sometimes, in the lane leading to the river, a tired cow would lie down and the other cows would spill sideways, break fences and trample the villagers' bean patches. Women rushed from their houses and shook their fists, but the riders took no notice: the cattle-men never seemed to notice gardens.

Francisco Manoel liked helping them winch the animals aboard the wherries. Then, after dark, he would listen to their stories of bandits and pumas. But if he asked to go along, someone was sure to say, 'The boy's too young,' and he went back to the hard bed and disapproving crucifix.

HE HAD MADE up his mind to run away when a rider came into town with news that his mother's old companion was dying at a ranch some leagues into the bush.

Outside the shack a sorrel stallion chomped at the hitching post. He pushed back the cowhide that served as a door and saw a shrunken figure laid out on a pallet. A crust of pustules covered his face and his eyes were closed.

Feebly, Manuelzinho gestured to his saddle, his quirt,

an ocelot waistcoat, a waterproof made of boa skin and a leather hat sewn with metal medallions.

'Take them,' he said.

The boy rode off with some passing horsemen. He did not say goodbye to the priest. Nor did he ever go back.

FOR THE NEXT seven years, he drifted through the backlands of the North-East, taking odd jobs as butcher's apprentice, muleteer, drover and gold panner. Sometimes he knew a flash of happiness, but only if it was time to be departing.

Duststorms burnished his skin. His clothes reeked of sour milk and horses. When drought tore at his throat, he soothed it with an infusion brewed from the tail of a rattle-snake.

Faces he forgot, but he remembered the sensations: the taste of the armadillo meat roasted in clay; the shock of aguardiente on the tongue; the pleasures of hot blood spurting over his hands, or of pissing down the leg of his horse.

He lived in Indian villages. He rode with gipsies who sold dud slaves and scapulars of St Anthony. For a season he washed gravel, working shoulder to shoulder with negroes, at a diamond-camp. It astounded him to find their fetor so exciting: he would compare their uncreased foreheads with the battle raging inside his own.

He knew he was brave. One night, a face loomed red in the firelight: he was amazed by the ease with which his knife slid into the man's belly. Another time, bivouacked on the Raso da Catarina, he shared his meat with a bush-wanderer whose clothes were a patchwork of green silk and whose fingers were stiff with gold rings. The man walked eighteen leagues a day, barefoot through the cacti:

'I trust no one,' he said. 'Why should I trust a horse?'

Not for months did Francisco Manoel realize that this was the bandit Cobra Verde who robbed only rich women and only for their finery.

And he too believed he would go on wandering for ever: yet, on Santa Luzia's Day of 1807 – a grey, stifling day that held out the promise of rain – the aimless journeys ended.

HE HAD BEEN riding through the village of Uauá when the potter's daughter rushed from her house with an apron-ful of green oranges. A week later he brought her trinkets: within a month they had married.

He found work on a ranch nearby. His employers were a family of absentee landlords called Coutinho, who had ranched in the Sertão for two centuries, but now lived on their sugar plantation by the sea.

He learned the equations of grass and water; the flight of birds around a stricken cow, or the presence of an underground spring. For leagues around he could distinguish all the neighbours' brands: it was a point of honour to return a lost animal no matter how far it had strayed.

Not far away, along the river-bed, there were cotton fields worked by poor sharecroppers. Knowing him to be cool and resourceful, they came to him when they were cheated and he would force the landowners to admit their miscalculations and pay up. But when the share-croppers came again, with gratitude and humble presents, a bitter taste rose up his throat, and he brushed them aside.

The Coutinhos paid no wages, but each round-up entitled the cowhands to one calf in four.

For two years he sold his animals, preferring coins in his pocket to wealth on the hoof. But for the third season he ordered a branding iron from the blacksmith and set about 'humanizing' his property.

He coralled young bulls, tied their legs and lashed them to a wooden post. He sliced off their testicles and sawed the tips of their horns. They slavered and moaned as the iron sizzled into their flanks: it gave him pleasure to rub the hot tallow into his own initials.

And he enjoyed his simple house with its gourds and melons straggling over the porch and its ochre walls that sucked up the sunlight. After a hard day he would unhook his guitar and strum the old songs of the Bandeirantes.

His wife dressed always in pink. She could sew, plant vegetables, cook, and squeeze the poisonous juice from manioc. Yet her movements were stiff and mechanical. Making love meant no more to her than sweeping the floor. A dazzling set of teeth froze the words in her throat. She would make her eyes glitter if she wanted something, or cloud them over if ever she was afraid. More often, she sat, staring into the distance, stroking an orange cat.

She would wake in the night and scream, 'Father! Father!' Twice a week she went to see the potter and came back red to the elbows in clay.

The strain of living with her told on his nerves. The sight of her vacant smile made him pale with anger and tempted him to sink his fingers in her throat. He took to sleeping rough, hoping to recover his equilibrium under the stars.

HE WOKE ONE sunrise on a patch of stony ground and, squinting sideways, was surprised to see, so far from water, a green frog crouching under the arm of a cactus. Its back was the colour of new grass, its belly mauve, and when it crawled, patches of orange and turquoise flashed from under its legs.

He poked the frog with a stick. It stiffened with fright. He watched its eyes suffuse from silver to purple. He took a stone and pounded it to a blood-streaked slime and, for a whole week, regretted what he had done.

His wife was expecting a child.

The women of the village came with advice, with bunches of rue to keep off witches, and a crucifix to place under the mattress. But the prospect of witnessing the birth disgusted him. He made an excuse to go on a journey and, afterwards, could never believe that the child, who curled her fingers round his, was his own daughter.

He was alone in the house one afternoon sewing a patch on a leather horse-frontal. Rain smacked on the rooftiles and cut winding channels in the earth. From time to time he looked up and watched the black clouds streaming past the window frame. Suddenly, the cat was sitting on the sill.

He went on sewing but the cat stared in his direction. When it miaowed, he felt as if a scalpel were scouring the inside of his skull. It bounded over and started sharpening its claws against his breeches. He shivered as its head nuzzled his calf. One hand reached under its forelegs, the other for a knife.

The blood was warm and sticky on his hands. He wiped the dark drops coagulating on the floor. He put the cat over his saddle and rode off to get rid of it. Then he stood for hours, hopelessly alone, in the cloudbursts.

The woman looked for the cat but soon forgot about it.

One evening she tucked the baby into her cradle and, balancing a waterjar on her head, went off to refill it at the tank. He watched them go, two undulating forms, receding down an alley of agaves into an orange sunset. He sat savouring the silence, and then began to twang at his guitar. The baby cried. He stopped playing and the baby stopped. But when he touched the strings again, the cries redoubled.

He held the guitar above the cradle, waited for the crash of splintering wood, then checked himself and broke it across his knee.

He had gone before the woman came back.

HE WENT BACK to his solitary wanderings. Believing any set of four walls to be a tomb or a trap, he preferred to float over the most barren of open spaces.

He passed through valleys of white dust where men in white went digging for tubers. Jerked beef was his food, dried fruits and wild honey: water he pressed from the roots of the umbu.

Sometimes there was water and no grass, but sharp sedges only and the horses falling from hunger. The journeys were endless, over empty horizons: the sound of hoofs on chips of silica, the crack of dead branches, the crack of rainless thunder, the shriek of a vulture – whatever broke the silence was sadder than silence.

And when he did go to the towns, the noises oppressed him: the dances, the music, the lively talk and laughter – he would crouch on his haunches and swig at a bottle.

And in the evenings he would stroll past houses and peer into the lamplit rooms, where fathers played with children, men played cards and women smiled as they braided their hair. He craved their simple pleasures of touch and trust; but if a woman saw the green eyes glinting in the darkness, she closed her shutters and bars of light slid through the jalousies and striped his face.

ONE LENT HE passed the sacred mountain, Monte Santo, where the Capuchin Father, Apollonio of Todi, found mysterious letters carved in rock.

Pilgrims in sky-blue rags came here from all parts of the Sertão to climb the white quartz *via sacra* to the chapel on the summit where, every Good Friday, the Virgin shed tears of blood.

He heard their litanies. He heard their cries as they flailed themselves with nettle-spurge. He watched them crawl the four miles on their kneecaps and the path becoming redder as they neared their goal.

He longed to perform some similar act of mortification, or simply to unburden his load. He would gaze for hours at wayside crosses. He never passed a village without dismounting to watch a congregation at prayer – yet he could never join them.

Once, at Jeremoabo, he stopped to speak to some women laying lilies on the altar. The guardian of the church was a young mulatto with skin-covered bones for legs, who propelled himself in a wood-wheeled cart, always looking over his shoulder as if someone, perhaps Death, were coming to collect him. He introduced the visitor to his companions: Santa Rosario in green lace; Sts Theatriel, Uriel and Barakiel; St Moses the Black with his foot on Pharaoh's windpipe; or St Anthony of Padua, whose tortured image would appear to runaway slaves and tell them to go home.

The cripple pushed himself up the aisle, unlocked the chest under the altar, and rolled back the shroud of mildewed velvet to uncover the cadaver of Christ.

The body was smooth and white, the belly taut, and the palms held inarticulately outwards. Black hair, graceful as a girl's, swirled about the shoulders. Red paint gushed from the lance wound and the knees were crimson scabs.

'Dead!' the cripple whimpered, and the tears welled up, out and round his cheeks, and pattered among the wreckage of his legs onto the boards of the cart.

Francisco Manoel laid a hand on the hunched shoulder. His mouth crinkled and he too, suddenly, burst out crying.

A cassock swished past.

He bolted for the door.

HE HAD NOT cried since before his mother's death: the tears relieved his sorrow. The fear that he would turn into a killer left him. He began to drink in bars, to laugh and play cards, though still he would not trust himself with a woman.

He was drawn towards the cities of the coast.

He went as far south as Tucano, where the cacti grew stunted and the big trees began, and where his old employer, Colonel Octávio Coutinho, owned a factory for making jerked beef. There, as if to purge himself in blood, he worked with the butchers and the salters, and would hang the slabs of meat to dry on copper wires. The grease boilers covered the town in a pall of smoke. Healthy men died of fever and the survivors drank.

From time to time caravans came up from the coast to buy beef for the slaves on the sugar estates. One January evening the Colonel's heir came to fetch a load for the family plantation at Tapuitapera: he had been sent along with the muleteers to toughen him up.

Joaquim Coutinho had dark wounded eyes that watered in the wind. His clothes were coated with a bloom of dust. His buttocks were in agony – he was unused to long journeys in the saddle – and the slave boys snickered as they watched him dismount.

That night he and the backlander struck up a friendship that could only be explained by the attraction of opposites. Next day, when the panniers were loaded and the men were ready to leave, Joaquim said he would like to stay on.

Francisco Manoel taught him to lasso steers, to braid rawhide whips, to break colts and ride down rheas and snare them with slingstones. Yet he, in turn, sat tongue-tied to hear Joaquim prattle of his lineage and latifundias, and of the Tower at Tapuitapera that had stood two hundred years.

One day, Joaquim said, 'You should ride with me down to the coast.'

He held back: secretly, he dreaded setting eyes on the sea.

Then he said, 'Yes.'

TAPUITAPERA, SO NAMED after a rock on which the Tapuya Indians once sharpened their axe-blades, was a hump of red sandstone about seventy miles north of Bahia and three miles inland from a beach of white sand. On the summit was the shadow of something dark and solid half-seen through the shining trees.

The sea was always blue and dotted with the sails of outriggers, and offshore breezes soughed through woods of mango and cashew trees.

The Coutinhos' plantation house had cross-lattice windows and walls of pink stucco. Green silk curtains rustled in its flower-stencilled apartments. On the verandah there were aviaries of song-finches; and in the dining room vases of blue-glazed porcelain, gilded pilasters and panels the colour of lapis lazuli.

The scents of rose and lily drifted through the garden.

Humming-birds sucked from scarlet honeysuckle. Morpho butterflies fluttered over the morning-glories and, after dark, in a Chinese loggia, black choirboys in snuff-velvet breeches and lace jabots would sing Pergolesi's *Stabat Mater*.

And Francisco Manoel imagined he had stumbled on Paradise.

The Colonel welcomed him as a good influence on his son, treated him as one of the family and put him in charge of his stables.

The Colonel was a magnificent wreck.

As a young man, frenzied at the thought of horizons unpopulated by his own cattle, he had extended his ranches into the green void of Maranhão, where horses sank to their withers and his ranch-hands died of anal gangrene. A parchment map of his empire still hung in his office. But his desk was stacked with copies of unpaid rent demands and, every month or so, word would come from some ranch upcountry that the tenant had annexed it.

Fifty years of peppery food and pitching in the saddle had so inflamed his haemorrhoids that he could move from his hammock neither to dine, to sleep, to shit, to pray nor play cards with his chaplain. His one pleasure was to have his hair washed by a lovely mulatta, who would run her fingers through the stiff waves as if peeling the outer leaves off a cabbage.

Francisco Manoel did his best to humour him. He put on freshly laundered whites for dinner. He took care to lose every other game of backgammon, and listened with attention to his stories of killing Indians.

The two young friends fought gamecocks and trained a pack of hounds to hunt for capybaras in the forest. Returning, hot from the chase, they would wave up to Joaquim's sisters, who lounged on feather hammocks or fed slips of custard-apple to their pet marmosets.

On rainy days they explored the Tower, a gloomy granite colossus built in 1602 by Francisco Coutinho the First, whose leathery face stared out from the walls of the portrait gallery.

Or they would leaf through volumes with vistas of European cities, or visit rooms where precious objects were strewn in disarray: Venetian glassware, silver from Potosí, crystal and cinnabar and black lacquer cabinets sloughing pearlshell.

Francisco Manoel could not account for what he saw. He had never thought of owning more than his knives and a few silver horse-trimmings. Now, there was no limit to his thirst for possessions.

IN MARCH THE time came round for the harvest. The hills and valleys flashed silver with the beards of sugar cane and, from the House, they could see lines of black backs and the glint of machetes. The blacks hacked at the wall of yellow stalks twice the height of themselves. The leaves slashed their skin and, by afternoon, the blood had mixed with the sweat and cane-juice and attracted swarms of flies.

A thick smell of molasses hung over the mill. Vats

bubbled. Pairs of yoked oxen turned the rollers of the cane press, and the slaves staggered towards it, bowed under the weight of the sheaves, with their neck-veins bulging.

One afternoon, a man got his hand caught in the rollers and the overseer had to hack it off at the wrist. His screams silenced the valley as his friends took him back to his cabin. The overseer shrugged and said, 'Not another!'

When the chapel bell clanked at six, the slaves downed tools and trudged uphill to say an evening prayer to the Virgin. They filed past the Colonel and raised their hats. Opaque, husky voices repeated his 'Boa Noite!' in unison.

The chapel was dedicated to Nossa Senhora da Conceiçao, and on the altar was the portable oratory of the Last Supper that would end its days at Ouidah. The nuns, who made it, had used as their model the dining room of the Big House. For some reason Francisco Manoel wanted to own it more than any other object he had seen.

LYING AWAKE ONE night, he heard a sound of drumbeats in the hills.

He dressed and followed the sound to a forest clearing where some slaves were calling their gods across the Atlantic. The dancers wore white metal masks and white dresses that glowed orange in the firelight. They whirled round and round until Exu the Messenger tapped them between their shoulder-blades. Then, one by one, they shuddered, growled, crumpled at the knees and fell to the ground in trance.

Their priest, a Yoruba freeman called Jerónimo, was a votary of Yemanja the Sea Goddess and he slept beside her mermaid image in a chamber bursting with corals and basins of salt water.

Nothing gave Francisco Manoel greater pleasure than to sit with this androgynous bachelor and hear him sing the songs of the Kingdom of Ketou in a voice that suggested, not the gulf between continents, but planets.

Jerónimo showed him the loko tree, sacred to Saint Francis of Assisi, whose writhing roots were said to stretch under the ocean to Itu-Aiyé, to Africa, the home of the Gods. Sometimes, a slave on the plantation would hear his ancestors calling through the rubbery leaves. At night he would creep among the branches and, in the morning, they would find the body, hanging.

Jerónimo told him stories of mudbrick palaces lined with skulls; of tribes who exchanged gold dust for tobacco; a Holy Snake that was also a rainbow, and kings with testicles the size of avocados.

The name 'Dahomey' took root in his imagination.

AND IT WAS time for him to move from Tapuitapera.

The Colonel was sick and bad-tempered, and Joaquim bored by his company. He would deliberately pitch the conversation above his head, only to stop himself and say, 'Now why am I telling you that?'

His mother, Dona Epiphania, hated to see her son mix with inferiors and took her meals alone. She was a big woman with blotchy skin, black wings on her upper lip, and teeth corroded to thin brown wafers. She kept a silver-handled whip in her embroidery basket and, while a slave girl circulated the air with a leafy branch, would sit on a reed mat and plan vengeance on her husband's mistresses.

She called Francisco Manoel 'The Catamite'.

When he first came to the house, Joaquim's sisters blew him kisses and signalled love-messages in the language of the fan. But soon, their mother encouraged them to pick on his weak points. They mimicked his accent. They mocked his efforts at conversation and would screech with laughter when he used a knife and fork. They said, 'We do have chairs, you know,' if he squatted on his hams. Often, as he entered the room, they would cry, 'Hurry! Hurry! It's the Brute!' and dash for the door in a rustle of taffeta.

One evening, Joaquim told him his father had had a stroke and that Dona Epiphania insisted he leave the house.

Their eyes met.

Francisco Manoel flushed with anger, but saw it was useless to argue and bowed his head.

HE WENT TO Bahia.

He drifted round the City of All the Saints in a suicide's jacket of black velveteen bought off a tailor's dummy. Flapping laundry brushed across his face. Urchins kissed him on the lips as their fingers felt for his pockets. His feet slipped on rinds of rotting fruit, and puffy white clouds went sailing past the bell-towers.

He would stroll down the cobbles of the Pelourinho to

watch the street-boys practise shadow-wrestling. The 'Beautiful Dog of the North' was a dyed blue poodle that played cards; and after dark there was always an excuse to let off fireworks.

His principal amusement was to follow funeral processions. One day it would be a black catafalque encrusted with golden skulls. The next, a sky-blue casket for a stillborn child, or a grey corpse wrapped in a shroud of banana leaves.

He lodged in a tenement in the Lower City and got a job with a man who sold the equipment of slavery – whips, flails, yokes, neck-chains, branding-irons and metal masks: the shop reminded him of tack-shops in the backlands.

His green eyes made him famous in the quarter. Whenever he flashed them along a crowded alley, some-one was sure to stop. With partners of either sex, he performed the mechanics of love in planked rooms. They left him with the sensation of having brushed with death: none came back a second time.

The lineaments of his face fell into their final form.

His right eyebrow, hitched higher than the left, gave him the air of a man amazed to find himself in a mad-house. A moustache curled round the sides of his mouth, which was moist and sensuous. For years he had pinched back his lips, partly to look manly, partly to stop them cracking in the heat: now he let them hang loose, as if to show that everything was permitted. The fits of anger had left him, not so the remorse. He wanted to go to Africa, but would not take a conscious decision.

Whenever a ship from Guinea anchored off the Fort of São Marcello, he would stroll round the slave quays and watch the blacks being rowed ashore. Dealers from every province elbowed forward, shouting themselves hoarse as they identified the consignors' brands. They calculated the numbers of the dead; then made the survivors run, stamp, lift weights and bellow to show the soundness of their lungs.

The defectives were sold off cheap to gipsies.

Francisco Manoel made friends with one of these gipsy slave-copers, who taught him some tricks of the trade: how to hide bloody dysentery with an oakum plug, or a skin disease by smearing it with castor oil.

But when he talked to old Africa hands, every one of them shuddered at the mention of Dahomey.

ONE DECEMBER AFTERNOON, for lack of anything better to do, he helped some hired ruffians hang a straw-filled effigy of the British Consul: it was four years since Parliament passed the Abolition Act, but only in recent months had the Royal Navy started seizing Brazilian slave ships.

The crowds worked themselves into a fury and, when a platoon of militia dispersed them, they set on a Scottish sailor and dumped him in the harbour. Perhaps Francisco Manoel's strongest memory of Bahia was of leaning over a balustrade and watching the red head bobbing amid a lattice of masts and spars.

A fortnight later, he was drinking a glass of sweet lime outside the slave auction on the Rua dos Matozinhos when one of the lot numbers, a Benguela houseboy, ran off in the middle of the bidding. Joaquim Coutinho was

74

among the buyers and, as the sales clerks chased the fugitive, he spotted his old friend and tapped him on the shoulder.

They renewed their friendship: in fact, whenever Joaquim came to town, the two would spend an evening together and a night with the whores.

On one of these visits, he said that the Colonel had died, leaving the family affairs in a terrible state, and forcing Dona Epiphania to sell her diamonds. Hoping to repair the fortune, he had joined a syndicate of army officers, whose aim was to corner the market in dried beef and invest the profit in faster slave ships.

The most valuable slaves came from Ouidah – and Ouidah, by terms of the Prince Regent's treaty with England, was the one port north of the Equator where it was legal to trade: the only problem was the King of Dahomey, who was mad.

Francisco Manoel made it clear he had only the haziest idea where Dahomey was.

'You should go there,' said Joaquim. 'You'd soon find out.'

THREE WEEKS LATER, Francisco Manoel found himself in a room at the Capitania, where the city's founding fathers peered from the dark panelling and Joaquim's partners were seated round a table.

A man in gold epaulettes and a red sash got to his feet, twirled a terrestrial globe, pointed to the Fort of St John the Baptist at Ouidah, and raised the candidate to the rank of lieutenant. The commission carried no salary, but came with two free uniforms, a passage to Africa and permission to trade in slaves. None of the officers knew what had happened to the Governor of the Fort, or to its garrison. At the end of the interview, everyone rose to their feet to congratulate the man they knew would be a corpse.

On his last night ashore, with the slaving brig *Pistola* stowed and ready for sea, he went to a farewell Mass at the Hospice of Boa Viagem.

The church was lit by a double row of crystal chandeliers and the walls were covered with panels of blue-and-white tiles. The tiles were painted with galleons – galleons dashed on rocks, toppled by waves, lashed by leviathans or battered in gunfights – yet always saved by the Blessed Virgin who hovered in an aureole above the masthead.

The captain and sailors sat in the front pews.

All were men with blood on their hands; yet all gazed longingly at the milk-white body of Our Dying Lord, identifying His Agony with their agony and calling on Him to pacify the sea.

The priest said a short prayer to the Patron of Slavers, St José the Redeemed, and a longer one for the souls of the Black Brethren who would be ransomed for the Christian fold. Nasal responses rose to the roof, where the Prophet Elijah, in spirals of smoke and flame, continued his chariot journey towards the Almighty.

Candles blazed on the altar, and the light flickered on the golden wings of angels.

From his seat at the back, Francisco Manoel saw the priest exhibit the ciborium and the crew file meekly towards him: *Corpus Domini Nostrum Jesum Christum . . . Corpus Domini Nostrum . . .* '

Without a second for reflection, he joined them – making a treaty with the hand in lace cuffs and letting the wafer wetten on the tip of his tongue.

Outside, the storm had blown over. Stars shrank and expanded in the blue void. Lightning flashed over the island of Itaparica, silhouetting the ship's yardarms out in the fairway.

The Mass ended, and the sailors stood outside the church holding up the ship's mizzen topgallant by its tack and clews. The choir sang an anthem and the priest's golden chasuble detached itself from the angels and was seen moving slowly down the aisle.

The procession passed through the green doors.

Boys in purple cassocks carried a silver cross, a stoup and a palm-frond aspergillum.

Drops of Holy Water pattered onto the canvas.

'Bless, O Lord, this ship *Pistola* and all who sail in her. Bear her as you bore the Ark of Noah over the flood-waters. Give them your hand as you gave it to the Apostle Peter when he walked upon the waters of the sea . . . '

FOUR

HE LANDED AT Ouidah between two and three of a murky May afternoon smelling of mangrove and dead fish. A band of foam stretched as far as the eye could reach. Inland, there were tall grey trees which, at a distance of three miles, anyone might mistake for waterspouts. He was the only passenger in the canoe: the crew knew better than to set foot in the Kingdom of Dahomey.

At the start of the voyage he had gazed at the new element with the innocent awe of the landsman. He saw boobies. He saw fleets of medusas, ribbons of sea-wrack, the prismatic colours on the backs of bonitos and albacores and the pale fire of phosphorescence streaming into the night.

Then, as the ship sailed into the horse-latitudes, the sails hung slack, shark fins swirled on an oily sea, everyone lost their tempers, and the mate smashed a sailor's teeth in with a marlinspike.

A shower of red rain spattered the deck the day they sighted the African coast, and a locust got caught in the rigging. On his last night aboard, Francisco Manoel woke up covered in his own vomit: the ship had narrowly missed the tornado that covered the shore with dead fish.

He brushed aside the krumen who helped him from the canoe. He refused to 'dash' the outstretched hand of the fetish-man. He refused to let the porters carry him across the lagoon, and with black ooze coating his thighs he strode up the track to the Captains' Tree.

Waiting in the shade of this decrepit ficus were some underlings of the Yovogan, the Dahomean Minister for the Slave Trade. Decanters of claret, madeira, rum and distilled palm-wine were laid out on a card table missing most of its baize.

He drank their toasts and soldiers fired their muskets in the air. A royal eunuch with silver horns on his temples tilted his head, asked what presents he had brought from Brazil, and gasped when the answer was 'None!'

A palaver followed, and everyone seemed quite friendly, but when he reached the Fort he found the place in ruins.

The flagstaff was broken, the Royal Arms defaced. Walls were roofless and smoke-blackened. The shutters were wrenched off their hinges and the cannon had come adrift of their emplacements and were sinking through the swish walls.

Turkey buzzards flapped off as he stepped into the yard. A pig was teasing the rind off a jackfruit. A dog pissed against a tree and started howling.

Through the door of the chapel came a gangling pox-pitted figure in a drum major's shako and the remains of a Turkish rug. He blinked at the newcomer; then, curling his lips back over a set of loose yellow teeth, whooped, 'Mother of Jesus Christ and All the Saints be praised!' and bounded over to paw the apparition and make sure it was real.

Taparica the Tambour was the only survivor of the garrison.

A Yoruba freeman who had joined the 1st Regiment of Black Militia, he told his sad story in the lilting cadences of plantation Portuguese: of how the Governor died of fever, the lieutenant in a skirmish by the shore; and how the King had let his soldiers loot the Fort.

They stole the bells, cut the eyes from the Prince Regent's portrait, unstoppered the rum barrels, buggered a cadet, and marched the men off to Abomey where, for all he knew, their heads were on the palace wall.

Thinking he knew the secret of buried treasure, the Dahomeans put ants on the Tambour's chest, pepper under his eyelids and burned his tongue with the tip of a red hot machete. They were about to do their worst when someone explored the powder magazine with a lighted firebrand. Seven bodies were taken from the wreckage, and they left him thereafter in peace.

In the last of the light he walked his rescuer round the garden where there were mounds of red earth, each set with a rough wood cross. Then they barricaded the gate with palm-trunks.

Francisco Manoel slung his hammock and lay under a muslin net listening to a symphony of frogs and mosquitoes. And he congratulated himself: for the first time in forty-seven days, he rocked to his own rhythm, not that of the ship.

AT SEVEN IN the morning the Yovogan's messenger came with an order for the Brazilian to present himself at once.

Taparica shook his head.

'King him need gun,' he said. 'Yovogan him come you.'

The Kingdom, it so happened, was passing through one of its periodic bouts of turmoil. The people had had enough of the King's blasphemous ways. He had failed to 'water', with blood, the graves of his ancestors. He was a coward and a drunk. Food was scarce, the army was out of ammunition while, from the east, the Alafin of Oyo was threatening to invade.

The messenger shouted abuse and went away, only to return with word of an official visit.

Puffs of musket smoke preceded the Yovogan, a frail octogenarian who rode to the Fort in a costume of pink satin, propped up by the grooms, sitting sidesaddle on a starved grey nag. A man led the beast by a grass halter. Another twirled a blue umbrella. A noisy entourage followed.

It was raining. Boys splashed alongside carrying the old man's cigar case, his stool, and the card table and decanters. Once inside the gate he signalled his wish to dismount, and the groom lifted him from the saddle, sat him down and removed his black tam-o'-shanter.

The Yovogan clicked his fingers in salutation, then proposed his own King's health in palm-wine and the Queen of Portugal's in Holland's Gin. He did not drink himself but poured the contents of both glasses down the gaping mouth of an acolyte.

The interview began in broken Portuguese. The Yovogan's face turned grey as he registered his disapproval at the lack of presents.

What about the barquentine full of silk? What about the coach and horses? Or the trumpets? Or the silver hunting-gun?

'There are no presents,' said Francisco Manoel.

'Not even the greyhounds?'

'Not even greyhounds.'

Nor would there be any presents, until the King released the prisoners, repaired the Fort and resumed the sale of slaves.

Everyone was confused, then angry. A man shouted, 'Death to Whites!' and an Amazon whirled her cutlass round her forefinger and brought it close to the Brazilian's face.

But when the Yovogan raised his hand, the crowd melted away muttering.

THAT SAME AFTERNOON, a hubbub of shouts and whip-lashes awoke Francisco Manoel from his siesta. Peering over the north bastion, he saw a crowd of naked men piling up bundles of reeds, planks, baskets of oyster shells and buckets of swish: the Yovogan had sent a corvée of captives to make good the damage.

In the weeks that followed Lieutenant da Silva worked in heat that would have driven most whites to their hammocks or their graves. Even on quivering after-noons, when the sun sucked out the colour of earth and leaves, he would strip to the waist, bark orders and shoulder the heaviest loads himself.

The blacks were amazed to see a white man work.

They thatched the roofs, whitewashed the walls and mucked out the cistern. Again the cannon gleamed with blacking and palm-oil. Again ships offshore saw the 'five shields' of the Braganzas floating from the flagpole, signalling that the Fort of St John the Baptist had slaves for sale.

The first batch were criminals convicted of stealing the

King's palm-nuts and condemned to be fed on them till they burst: none seemed the least unhappy to be leaving Dahomey.

More slavers came – the *Mithridate*, the *Rinoceronte*, the *Fraternidade* and the *Bom Jesus* – each carrying crates of muskets, rum, tobacco, silks and calico. The Alafin of Oyo did not invade. The King went to war against some defenceless millet planters in the Mahi Mountains and, within two years, Francisco Manoel had sent no less than forty-five slave cargoes to Bahia.

Joaquim Coutinho had the sense to offer him a place in the syndicate.

DA SILVA TOOK to the Trade as if he had known no other occupation. Having always thought of himself as a foot-loose wanderer, he now became a patriot and man of property. No word of congratulation came from his superiors in Bahia. Yet he believed it was his heaven-sent vocation to fuel with black muscle the mines and planta-tions of his country, and he believed they would reward him.

He persisted in this illusion with the obstinacy of the convert. Often on sleepless nights he would lie and listen to the groan and clank of the barracoon, only to re-member the sweet singing in the chapel at Tapuitapera and roll over with his conscience clean.

He lived in the Governor's suite of rooms; he restored the chapel and imported a Portuguese padre to say Mass before the start of each voyage.

As major-domo of the Fort, Taparica dressed in a green frock-coat, sailor pants of white canvas and a black felt bicorn with a cockade of parrot plumes. Whenever they passed through the town, he would stride ahead of the hammockeers, clanging an iron bell and shouting, '*Ago! Ago!*' to clear the path.

He slept on a mat outside his master's room. He cooked and tasted his food, controlled his drinking habits and emptied his slop-pail. He found girls for his bed, aphrodisiacs if the weather was exceptionally sticky, and warned him not to make lasting attachments.

Francisco Manoel would use the same girl for a night or two, then send her home with a present for her family.

His profits – and reputation for straight dealing – exasperated the veterans of the Trade. One year, a Captain Pedro Vicente begged him for a shipload of slaves without money or goods to pay. He swore to return but squandered the proceeds in Bahia and did not come back. Some time later, on hearing that the same man was in Lagos with an unseaworthy ship and a mutinous crew, Da Silva sent his cutter with a message: 'Come over to Ouidah and I will refit you. Nobody cheats me twice.'

Nor was he less straightforward in his dealings with the King.

The two men never met: a taboo forbade Dahomean monarchs setting eyes on the sea. But if the King wanted twelve gilt chairs, they were sent. If he wanted twenty plumed hats, these were found. And he even got his greyhounds, which came specially from England – though, on their way up to Abomey, the dog was bitten by a rabid bitch.

Every month or so an invitation came for Francisco

Manoel to visit the capital. He would read each letter through and politely decline: on the first one, the King's Portuguese scribe had written a warning in the margin:

'I, Antonio Maciel, have been sixteen years a prisoner of this cruel king without seeing another of my country-men . . .'

THE KING WENT to war in January and the chain-gangs started reaching Ouidah towards the end of March.

The captives were numb with fright and exhaustion. They had seen their homes burned and their chiefs slaughtered. Iron collars chafed their necks. Their backs were striped purple with welts; and when they saw the white man's ships, they knew they were going to be eaten.

The Dahomeans' mindless cruelty offended Da Silva's sense of economy. Time and again, he complained to the Yovogan that the guards were ruining valuable property, but the old man sighed and said, 'It is their custom.'

On arriving at the Fort, the slaves were housed in a long shed, roofed with dried grasses and fenced in with a palisade of sharpened stakes. Each was manacled to an iron chain that ran in bights down the length of the structure. The thatch came lower than a man's waist and, when the buyers peered in out of the sunlight, all they could see were eyes in the darkness.

Every morning, after the Angelus, they were fed from a cauldron of millet gruel and driven to the lagoon where they washed and danced for exercise.

Taparica cured the sick and calmed their fears: in a dozen dialects he would burble of their country-to-be where everyone danced and cigars grew on trees. He taught his master to distinguish the various tribes by their cicatrices. He could tell any man's age by the state of his gums; and if in doubt, would lick his cheeks to test the resilience of his stubble.

The loading was done in the cool of the evening, when the sea was down – the same scene repeated year after year: the ship, the waves, the black canoes, the black men shorn of their breechclouts, and the slave-brands heating in driftwood fires.

Francisco Manoel preferred to do the branding himself, taking care to dip the red-hot iron in palm-oil to stop it sticking to the flesh.

The chains were struck off at the water's edge, so that, in the event of capsize, one man would not drag the others down. Only occasionally, in a final bid for freedom, would one fling himself to the breakers; if, later, his shark-torn carcass was washed ashore, Taparica would bury it in the dunes, sighing, '*Ignorantes!*'

FIVE YEARS WENT by, of heat and mist and rain. The British stopped recognizing Ouidah as a slave port; and when a frigate of the West Africa Squadron boarded the brig *Borboleta*, becalmed off Ouidah with five hundred slaves aboard, Da Silva watched the fight through his telescope and said, 'At least something has happened.'

Often the Brazilian captains had to wait weeks

before the coast was clear but their host spared no expense to entertain them. His dining room was lit with a set of silver candelabra; behind each chair stood a serving-girl, naked to the waist, with a white napkin folded over her arm. Sometimes a drunk would shout out, 'What are those women?' and Da Silva would glare down on the table and say, 'Our future murderers.'

The sight of white men disintegrating in the tropics disgusted him. How he hated their hollow laughter! And as their warted contours dissolved behind clouds of cigar smoke, he would make an excuse to slip away and be alone.

On Thursdays he put on his regimentals and went to dine with the Yovogan in an open courtyard frescoed with ochre chameleons.

The old man was so old he could remember the piles of skulls put up to celebrate the Dahomean conquest of Ouidah in 1741 – and, to amuse his guest, would croak a refrain about using the dead king's head as a mortar:

Doli dohò mè sè
Boli sà boli sè

He liked his white friend so much that he took him to his bed-chamber to show off his blunderbuss and the nine rosaries of human molars, the souvenirs of his bloodthirsty youth. But he was equally fond of his European presents – the porcelain teapot of the Brandenburgers or the cruet-stand presented by the Royal Africa Company – since they reminded him of the days when ships of every nation crowded the roadstead.

The Yovogan trembled at the mention of the King's name. But one day, he unwrapped a framed engraving of the guillotine in the Place de la Concorde, the parting gift of Citizen-Governor Deniau before he left for France.

The idea of chopping off a king's head in public struck the old man with the force of a revelation. Deniau had explained that a tyrant forfeits the right to live, and, though he never understood the logic of that argument, it was an awesome precedent.

AND DA SILVA was always dreaming of Bahia. Whenever a ship sailed, he would watch the yardarms vanish into the night, then light a pipe on the verandah and sink into a reverie of the future: he would have a Big House, a view of the sea, grandchildren and the sound of water tinkling through a garden. But then the mirage would fade. The sound of drumbeats pressed against his temples and he had a presentiment that he would never get out of Africa.

He confided his fears to no one. To convince himself they were unreal, he would sit, red-eyed into the night, writing letters to Joaquim Coutinho, tearing up sheet after sheet in an effort to express himself:

These people must be the biggest thieves in the world. I would live on any other continent but this one. I would live in the lands of ice and snow, anywhere to be away from their gibberish . . .

Or:

I cannot begin to describe this cretinous existence of mine. Nor how lonely it is to be without family or friends. Perhaps next year I shall come back and marry . . .

He pleaded for news, any scrap of news, to keep his memories of Brazil from fading: but Joaquim's replies were invariably cold and commercial:

By our brig *Legitimo Africano* I have this day received your consignment of 230 items (144 M 86 f), also 41,500 cola nuts (female). I regret to report losses of one third owing to an outbreak of the bloody flux. I would like your opinion as to why the females do so much better than the males. In the meantime the above items will be sold for the highest possible price and your share returned in flintlocks, tobacco and iron bars . . .

But why, his partner wrote back, had they not made him Governor of the Fort? How he longed for one word that they were aware of his existence! 'My conduct, I can assure you, is irreproachable.'

The officers had not forgotten him. But since they were profiting, privately, from his activities, public recognition was out of the question.

At an official level, the Fort at Ouidah had ceased to exist.

GRADUALLY AFRICA SWAMPED him and drew him under. Perhaps out of loneliness, perhaps in despair of fighting the climate, he slipped into the habits of the natives.

He wore long pantaloons instead of the breeches that

gave him prickly heat in the groin. He wore amulets against the Evil Eye. Taparica taught him to shuffle his feet at the phallus of Papa Legba and, together, they went to the diviners.

The fear of illness obsessed him. But since his servant was an adept in the mysterious medicine of excrements, and since he trusted him in everything, he had no choice but to swallow his own piss for a liver attack; piss and yams for malaria; and when he had a sore throat, he would say a prayer to St Sebastian and flavour his coffee with fowl droppings.

Some evenings they went to the Python Temple to watch the novices sink their teeth into the necks of living goats. The spectators screamed with laughter as boys somersaulted on one another's backs and mimicked the motions of sodomy. When the lightning danced, the votaries of the Thundergod would axe their shoulder blades, then writhe and rear their buttocks to the sky.

He never knew what drew him to the mysteries. The blood? The god? The smell of sweat or the wet glinting bodies? But he was powerless to break his addiction and, realizing that Africa was his destiny, he took an African bride.

HER NAME WAS Jijibou.

She was sixteen.

Dehoué, her father, was a chief of the krumen, whose one ambition was to possess a white son-in-law. He had come four times to the Fort to propose yet another of his daughters. When turned down a fourth time, he had threatened to go on strike: the Yovogan said it was most insulting to refuse an offer of wives.

One December evening, Dehoué came again, this time with musicians and a figure muffled in white cloth. The town was silent but for the howl of breakers on the bar. Swifts were slicing the green air. The girl brushed past the spectators and tore off her veil.

She had owl eyes, a pouting mouth and shell-pink fingernails that fluttered at her finger-tips. Gold hoops shone in her ears. Her neck was a perfect cylinder. Her legs gleamed like metal rods and her torso, clad only in an indigo loincloth, was hard yet flexible as a hinge.

Her shoulders shuddered at the first roll of drums. Then she spun round. She pirouetted. She strutted. Her arms pumped the air, her feet kicked the dust. Sweat poured from her breasts and a musky perfume gusted into the Brazilian's face: not once did she let her gaze fall away from him.

The drummers stopped.

She stood before him, on tiptoe, swaying her hips and languidly laying out her tongue. Her arms beckoned. She bent at the knees. Then she arched her spine and bent over backwards till the back of her head brushed the ground.

Francisco Manoel caught her father's eye and nodded.

TAPARICA RATTLED HIS teeth with horror, said, 'You not know this people,' and moped about in a sulk. But Da

Silva put his reaction down to jealousy and went ahead with plans for the wedding.

That midnight he left her panting behind the bed-curtains and chucked the red rag to the crowd of her relatives who had drunk far more rum than he had bargained for.

In the morning, Taparica prayed the blood came from his master's scratched and bleeding face, but his hopes fell on hearing the guffaws of the bride's mother as she inspected the night's work.

As for Francisco Manoel, he welcomed the change. The south-west angle of the Fort now echoed with the thumping of mortars and the ivory merriment of ripe women. He liked Jijibou's peppery messes. He liked twisting his tongue round the dissonant syllables of Fon. And when he loved her, she would rub her calloused heels, one after the other, down the depression of his spine.

She tightened her lips if ever he tried to kiss them. Yet her nostrils would quiver with pleasure at the sight of a new present. She would swan about begging approval for a new bandanna of Cantonese silk: what the eye saw, the fingers grabbed and played with, childishly.

One Thursday he gave her a Dutch looking-glass and she stared at herself, tossing her head this way and that way till Saturday, till she let it slide to the floor and shiver to bits.

Her stomach swelled and she gave birth to a boy the colour of pink coral. They called him Isidoro and the midwives buried his umbilical cord under the roots of a baobab.

But the delivery of a male heir was the signal for her relatives to move in. Not a day passed without some new cousin requiring to be fed. Jijibou stole the key to the liquor store and gave it to her brothers. He asked her to restrain them, but she said, 'Stealing from a white man isn't stealing.' And when he complained to the Yovogan, the old man looked dreamily over the chameleons and said, 'It is their custom.'

Late one night, they heard howls coming from the Yovogan's compound. He had died of delirium and the body had swelled up and gone green. Taparica knew which particular cactus had provided the poison, said it had 'not taste' and begged his master board the Brazilian brig at anchor in the roads.

But Francisco Manoel was unwilling to abandon his property.

THERE WERE BAD days ahead: the King had fresh troubles and was blaming them on the foreigners.

He replaced the Yovogan with a Commander of the Atchi Brigade, a man all mouth and no neck to speak of, who, at their first meeting, kept the Brazilian waiting five hours hatless in the sun. When asked to settle the King's debt, the man folded his arms and said, 'Dahomeans never sell slaves to white men.'

Within a month only a few cripples could be seen hobbling round the barracoon. People shut the doors in Da Silva's face. Boys darted across his path shouting, 'Road closed to whites!' The officials made him pay a toll to go down to the beach and a far bigger toll to come back. One morning, a headless black cock appeared on the altar of the chapel.

'Life here', he wrote to his partner, 'is not what it was a year ago, when a delicious life cost us nothing and we made good money. We are subject to the most humiliating searches and the Blacks are full of envy and hatred for the Whites. In addition, our friend the King of Dahomey has turned robber. He buys but does not pay. He owes me for the rifles of the *Atalante*, for the whole cargo of the *Flor da Bahia*, and hasn't sent one captive to the coast in nine months. I cannot say what I should do. Perhaps I should move to Badagry and trade with the King of Oyo? My man Fernandinho will tell you all, for he has been one of the victims . . . '

But Fernandinho did not get aboard with the letter. The customs men stripped him of all he possessed before they allowed him to board. And ten days later – the time it took to have the handwriting deciphered – a detachment of soldiers arrested Francisco Manoel and hauled him before the new Yovogan.

The rain had fallen all day and, all over town, naked men were lathering each other in the purplish puddles. In the outer yard some boys were sorting cowries into grass-cloth bags. He heard a raucous cry. A weight pressed on his shoulders. The last thing he remembered was a foot rammed hard against his windpipe.

He recovered consciousness lying in the mud with a red film covering his eyes: his head had hit the rim of a mortar as he fell. His right hand had swollen solid, where they had wrenched off the ring of his Brazilian marriage. Then they hobbled him with chains and put him in a stinking hut.

The guards pinched him, pulled his hair and kicked him in the kidneys. Pus oozed from the head wound. He dribbled dysentery. The small boys laughed.

97

He lost all sense of time and waited for death as one waits for a friend. Instead a messenger came with orders to take him to the capital.

HIS MEMORIES OF the journey melted into a colourful blur.

For seven days he tossed in his hammock, feverishly eyeing the runnels of sweat that poured from his bearer's back. At one village there were heads on poles: at another, women pointed up a tree to where a crucified man croaked for water in a library of sleeping fruit bats. Crossing the Great Marsh, there were weedy meres where red birds perched on dead branches and blue dragon-flies darted over the nenuphars. A porter missed his footing on the causeway and the mud peeled from his thighs in thick grey flakes.

It was night when they came into Abomey.

THE PALACE OF Abomey had tall walls made of mud and blood but very few doors. It lay at a distance of twenty-three thousand, five hundred and two bamboo poles from the beach. In its innermost compound lived the King, his eunuchs and three thousand armed women.

The guards put their prisoner to lodge in a low thatched house. When his strength returned, they took him for walks about the city, but the drumbeats, the headless victims, and stench of putrefaction made him dizzier and dizzier and he had to go back to his bed.

Sometimes the King passed by on the far side of the wall, but all Da Silva saw was a white parasol frilled with jawbones. He asked, 'When will I see the King?' and the guard lowered his eyelids and drew his forefinger across his Adam's apple.

Then, one morning at cockcrow, three eunuchs came and told him to dress. Hardly daring to look right or left, he followed their swishing orange robes through court-yards crammed with hollering tribesmen: everywhere an architecture of white skulls outnumbered the heads of the living.

They came into the presence of the King.

The King lay lounging on a bolster of carmine velvet, thronged by naked women, who fanned him with ostrich feathers and wiped the perspiration from his forehead.

He was a tall sinewy man with dry red eyes, automatic gestures and the bonhomie of the seasoned slaughterer. The rising sun shone on his chest. His fingernails curled like cocks' feathers. His loincloth was purple and his sandals were of twisted gold wire. At his feet were the heads of a boy and girl, sent half an hour earlier to tell the Dead Kings that their descendant had woken up. He glared at the Brazilian and spat.

All the commoners lay on the ground and, when he lifted his baton, they rubbed their noses in the dirt and bellowed, 'Dada! Breathe for me! Dada! Steal from me! Dada! Dada! Break me! Take me! My head is yours!'

A troubadour crawled forward, pointed at Da Silva, and said in a hollow voice, 'The bird who leaves her nest cannot carry away the eggs.'

An albino dwarf jumped up, saluted crazily, screeched

white man's talk and gurgled as if he were being garrotted.

The executioner ran his fingers up and down his knife-
blade.

But the prisoner knew better than to show fear and, as
if by suction, drew the monarch's mouth into a cracked
tobacco-stained smile.

By the end of the audience he was the King's friend.

NOT THAT HE was set free, merely that swarms of people
clustered round his house – to see him, to feel him, to
beg for medical treatment and give him food. Ministers
came to call, princes came. A man came with a tumour
the size of a loaf, and a woman kept coming with fruit and
said, 'I am your mother.'

He found the Portuguese prisoners and noted down
their names: 'Luis Lisboa . . . Antonio Pires . . . Roque
Dias de Jordão . . . ' but when he tried to get them released, the King said, 'You are my friend. Don't speak
about my enemies.'

The King said he loved him 'too much' and made him
stand at his side to watch every ceremony of importance.
So, Francisco Manoel saw the Horse Sacrifice and the
Platform Sacrifice, at which the victims were trussed in
baskets and toppled to the executioners. He saw the
spirits of Dead Kings moving with the slow disjointed
gait of skeletons. He saw the Dead Queen Mothers, who
were much more colourful and lively; the King's 'Birds'
who twittered and wore white, and the Lady Pipe
Smokers who looked rather ill.

Often, the King would dance himself, rolling his scapulars and weaving his steps around the skulls of his favourite victims. Or he would amuse himself by teaching little boys to chop heads, and when they made a mess of it shout, 'Not that way, you fool! Think of chopping wood!'

Then he would nudge his friend in the ribs and bellow, 'Ha! Whiteman! I drink from your head also.'

The courtiers cackled at his buffooneries, and Francisco Manoel wondered where the farce would end.

YET HE WAS not alone; for there was a young man who kept trailing him wherever he went.

His forehead was high and wide, his eyebrows were glistening arches and his teeth shone. He wore an iron ring on his upper arm. A pink tunic, slit at the sides, revealed the slabs of his back and chest, and a hunter's knife hung loosely from his belt.

His one defect was a cast in the right eye, which was veiled and bloodshot.

He seemed to be signalling a message, but when Francisco Manoel returned the smile, the face collapsed in idiotic blankness.

A guard said he was Kankpé, the King's mad half-brother.

A friendlier guard whispered that Kankpé was only shamming madness; that he was the rightful king, and only waiting for an omen to raise the rebellion.

IN APRIL, THE month when purple arums reared their hoods in the yamfields, there were fresh rumours spreading through the city.

The diviners who foresaw the future in egg-yolks and the surface of water were predicting catastrophe or change. At Sado, a woman gave birth to a boy who was half a leopard. The war against the Egbas had produced a total of five captives – and the King's behaviour had surpassed even Dahomean limits of tolerance.

He had tied up his two chief ministers, the Mingan and Meu, and spat rum in their faces. He had castrated a soldier whose hips were too wide. His sons had defiled a royal tomb, and he had opened the belly of one of his wives to prove her foetus was a boy.

One morning levée, an old man pushed through the crowd and raised a finger at the throne. His cheeks were hollow. His chest was smeared with white paste and white rags hung limply from his hips.

'Who are you?' asked the King.

'Can you not recognize Adjaholanhoun?' the man answered. 'It was I who obeyed your orders to poison your father. Now the Dead Kings have put me in prison for helping your crimes.'

The King shuddered and called for food for the stranger. But the old man threw the cornpastes over his left shoulder and said, 'The Dead eat so.' Then he poured the palm-wine over his right shoulder: 'The Dead drink so.'

The crowd parted, he walked into the mist and no one could find a trace of his footfalls.

All through that month the hyenas came into the streets at night and the city was silent by day. The King had played with his prisoner for a season and now had grown tired of his plaything. And the prisoner looked on death as a face unfolding from a mirror: he let himself hang limp when they dragged him out and threw him on the ground before the throne.

The King stood over him, his shadow falling in a dark diagonal stripe:

'Why has Portugal sent three hundred and thirty-five ships to attack Ouidah?'

'It hasn't.'

'Why did you kill my greyhound?'

He opened his mouth to speak, but the guards stoppered it with a wooden gag.

'So you think you're a white man?' the King sneered, and ordered him off to prison.

THE GUARDS SHAVED his head and dipped him in a vat of indigo.

To made sure the dye reached every pore, they made him submerge his head and breathe through a straw. They dipped him five times in a single moon, but each time, when they scrubbed him, the skin showed up grey underneath and they put him back to soak.

Then, since there was no precedent for beheading a white man – and since white was the colour of death and all whites were half-dead anyway – they left him to die without water or shade or food.

His legs withered. His stomach stretched taut as a drum. His skin erupted in watery pustules: whichever way he turned was agony. Phosphorescent centipedes crawled over him at night; and the vultures spattered him with ammoniac droppings, shuffling for position along the wall, and flexing their pinions with the noise of tearing silk.

He dreamed of walking through a line of airless rooms and, in each room, seeing his own head, crawling with meatflies, laid out on a silver dish. His fingers would push back the eyelids and a green light would flash and set the flies buzzing till they dropped, *ping . . . ping . . .*, and exploded in wisps of smoke.

Sometimes he saw Prince Kankpé, standing full-face as if frescoed on the wall, smiling and showing the gap between his two front teeth.

Memories of Brazil kept passing before his eyes: the miserable mud house, the pendulum of his dead mother's leg, the cries of his child, the penitents at Monte Santo, the treasures of the Coutinhos – and as he counted the wrong turnings that had brought him to this end, he choked with self-pity and promised to take the cowl if ever he got out of Africa.

Or he would shriek with laughter at the absurdity of dying in this charnel-house, where the dead were more alive than the living.

And when death came, it came quietly, at night. It loosed his chains and lifted him gently up a ladder, up and over the prison wall and laid him on cushions below.

Kankpé had stolen the wickerwork litter used for carrying cowrie-shells to count the annual census. No one, not even a customs officer, was allowed to look inside. The bearers headed north-west and had crossed the frontier before the alarm went up.

FRANCISCO MANOEL WOKE from his drugged sleep and let his eyes wander over the chaff-flecked walls of a mud hut. A cock crowed. He heard the burble of women's laughter and, from over the valley, the trills of a flute.

A shadow passed across the door, and a grey-haired man came in with a calabash of foaming milk. The foam stuck to his beard; he wiped it with his arm and went back to sleep.

Later, the same man revealed the identity of his rescuer: he was to wait in the village till Kankpé could join him.

He went for walks in the sere rolling hills where long-horned cattle were grazing. Far to the west an escarpment crinkled the horizon into facets of purple and blue. The land reminded him of the Sertão, but here the thorn-trees had orange bark and the thorns were long and white and seemed to be shining.

He woke one morning to hear news that Kankpé was hunting in the bush not far away. He walked with the boy till sunset, till they came to a water-gourd poised by the roots of a tree.

They heard him before they saw him, striding through the grass-blades. A freshly killed antelope widened the trapeze of his torso: a breechclout of brown leather merely emphasized his nakedness.

Kankpé flayed the animal in the half-light, throwing

105

the fat to the dog and burying the entrails so the soul should rest in peace. Then they ate the meat, grilled over a grid of green saplings.

A leopard barked in the bushes. He crawled to the edge of the clearing and barked back, and for a second they saw the spotted face flickering in the firelight.

'My father,' he said, and stretched out to sleep.

For the next five days they went out hunting together, feeling for affinities to break the lines of colour and custom.

Kankpé showed him the spoor of various antelopes – gazelles, kobs, waterbuck, guibs and bubals. He would steal up on a herd, now running, now crawling, now freezing motionless as an anthill if an animal reared its snout to sniff the wind. He would plunge into a marsh to drive out a wart-hog, or clamber up a tree to keep clear of a buffalo. He never threw his spear unless certain of his target. He despised the hunting gun as the weapon of a coward.

ON THE FIFTH night they swore a blood pact.

The moon in its final quarter smeared its light over the lumpy trunk of a baobab. Somewhere a hornbill rattled its beak and, not far off, there was a jackal howling.

The two men knelt facing each other, naked as babies, pressing their thighs together: the pact would be invalid if their genitals touched the ground.

The moon glinted on the black thighs and biceps, but white skin absorbs the moonlight evenly.

Kankpé fumbled in a leather bag and took out a skull-cup. He set it in the space between their knee-caps and added the ingredients of the sacrament: ashes, beans, baobab pith, a thunderstone, a bullet taken from a corpse, and the powdered head of a horned viper.

He half-filled the skull with water. Then they split each other's fingers and watched the black blood fall.

They drank in turn, running their tongues over the bullet and thunderstone.

Kankpé rolled his eyes and muttered curses: '*A dâ la* . . . *A dâ la* . . . ': blood-brothers live together and together they must die.

Francisco Manoel drank with the light-heartedness of the man who has skipped from certain death. It took another thirty years for him to realize the extent of his obligations.

FIVE

He made his way to the coast at Anecho, a slave port to the west of Ouidah in the territory of the Popos. The factory beside the lagoon belonged to a Mr George Lawson, a hunchback mulatto and son of an English captain called George Law. The house was still full of English knick-knacks, but the English ships no longer came and guinea-fowl had nested in the saloon.

He wanted to get out, to forget, to begin again. He would scan the horizon with Mr Lawson's telescope, watching for a blur to break into the two half circles of grey, but a ship was a long time coming. In the evenings he played chess, and the stories he told about Abomey distracted his partner from his moves.

At last, an old felucca flying Portuguese colours dropped anchor and sent a boat ashore. She was bound from Lagos to Bahia but a storm had washed her water-kegs overboard and she needed replacements. The Captain agreed to take him: the crew took him for yet another madman in an African port.

On his last night ashore, he could not sleep for thinking of Bahia. Already he saw the harbour, and the churches and the grog-shops of the waterfront. But towards daybreak he remembered he would be going back a pauper. He remembered his promise to help Prince Kankpé and, by morning, he was in the mood for revenge.

His letter to Joaquim Coutinho made light of his sufferings and told the syndicate of their chance to rid

111

Dahomey of a monster and replace him with a candidate of their own.

THE SYNDICATE REPLIED with a shipment of muskets, rum and tobacco. Teams of porters met Prince Kankpé's partisans on the frontier. A length of scarlet silk, torn into pennons, became the symbol of the revolt.

Francisco Manoel waited and went on playing chess: he had just begun a game with Mr Lawson when the new King's messenger burst into the saloon and blurted out the news.

Not five days before, the two Chief Ministers had attended the levée, but instead of grovelling and throwing dust on their heads, shouted, 'The Dead Kings have deposed you!' and each removed one of the golden sandals that only a King could wear.

The King winced at his ancestors' verdict, abdicated and allowed himself to be shut up in prison – where he would linger on another forty years, ordering imaginary executions and slumped in a torpor of compulsive eating.

Mr Lawson spat out the tamarind pod he had been chewing and said:

'All Dahomeans are liars and new King will be bad king same as old one.'

Francisco Manoel shuddered at the thought of Abomey and refused to leave with the messenger. More messengers came, offering honours and a monopoly of the Slave Trade. Again he refused.

112

Nor would he relent until the evening a black canoe came gliding through the fishweirs and grounded at Lawson's Landing. A leggy figure stepped ashore. It was Taparica.

Master and servant flew along the path and smothered each other in an embrace that astonished both of them. They talked all night and, though their talk was unexhausted by the morning, Taparica convinced him he had nothing to fear.

The bearers brought up his hammock; yet, as he lay down, Francisco Manoel turned to his host and said:

'You'll see. One day I shall end up his slave.'

.

THEY PASSED THROUGH the West Gate of Abomey, riding in an open landau hauled not by horses, but men. A twenty-one gun salvo was fired off. Umbrellas were broken in the crush.

The new King stood smiling to greet them in a toga of grey silk slashed with silver crescents: around his neck there was a single blue glass bead. He seemed to have grown taller and now trod the earth as if honouring it with his footfalls. He guided them to some chairs, thanked Taparica for 'landing the Big Fish', and, without warning, invested Francisco Manoel with the regalia of a Dahomean chief.

The clamours of the crowd increased in volume: '*Viva o amigo do Rey.*'

At sunset the King took them to a fortress where, peering from a platform, they saw the deposed monarch, reeling drunkenly round the yard, spitting balls of phlegm into the dust.

The King said:

> The hyena howls
> The elephant goes by

— and from that hour the Dahomeans called Francisco Manoel Adjinakou the Elephant.

WITHIN A YEAR he was the King's Viceroy at Ouidah and had turned Dahomey into the most efficient military machine in West Africa.

As long as he stayed on the coast, he assumed the manners and style of a Brazilian seigneur. From Cape Verde to the Bonny River, drifters of every colour came to feed at his table and test the resources of his cellar. Though the title 'Dom' was usually reserved for members of the Portuguese Royal Family, everyone called him 'Dom Francisco'.

He gave Ouidah the air of a civilized town by ordering drains to be dug and streets cut through its maze of pestilential alleys. He planted oil palms and coconuts, and introduced the pineapple. The flatlands were a sea of maize and manioc, and there were rice-paddies along the lagoon.

Because he forbade the lash on his plantations, his own workers adored him. On their way to the fields, they would file past his window and chant his litany:

The Elephant spreads his net
On land and sea
He buys mothers, fathers, sons
And the hyena howls in vain
Friends gather round the smells of his kitchen
Monkeys dance when they drink palm wine
He is the Good Sponge who sponges us clean
He hardens his walls with fire
He gives us pearls when we give him a mosquito
In one day he sold all the slaves in Ouidah
His well will never run dry.

No CAPTAIN COULD evade the vigilance of his coast-guards. None could load a slave without paying an export tax, or land a bale of cotton without paying him a due. His promissory notes were honoured by bankers in New York or Marseille. Alone or in partnership, he commissioned a fleet of Baltimore clippers.

These new ships were designed to out-tack any cruiser of the Royal Navy. They had tall raking masts, sleek black hulls, and he named them after seabirds: *Fregata, Albatroz, Gaivota, Alcatraz,* or *Andorinha-do-Mar.*

But they sailed at a sharp angle of keel: even in a moderate sea, the crew had to batten the hatches and close the gratings. The temperature in the hold shot up, and the cargoes died, from heat, from dysentery and lack of air.

Like every self-respecting slaver, he blamed his losses on the British.

EACH YEAR, WITH the dry season, he would slough off the habits of civilization and go to war.

His first task had been to reform the Dahomean army. He and the King got rid of the paunchy, the panicky and the proven drunks. And since Dahomean women were far fiercer fighters than the men – and could recharge a muzzle-loader in half the time – they sent recruiting officers round the villages to enlist the most muscular virgins.

The recruits were known as the 'King's Leopard Wives'.

They ate raw meat, shaved their heads and filed their teeth to sharp points. They learned to fire from the shoulder not the hip, and never to fire at rustling leaves. On exercises they were made to scale palisades of prickly pear, and they would come back clamouring, 'Hou! Hou! We are men!' – and since they were obliged to be celibate, were allowed to slake their lusts on a troop of female prostitutes.

Dom Francisco insisted on sharing all the hardships of the march.

He crossed burning savannahs and swam rivers infested with crocodiles. Before an attack on a village, he would lash leaves to his hat and lie motionless till cockcrow. Then, as the dawn silhouetted the roofs like teeth on a sawblade, a whistle would blow, the air fill with raucous cries and, by the end of the morning, the Amazons would be parading before the King, swinging severed heads like dumb-bells.

116

Dom Francisco greeted each fresh atrocity with a glassy smile. He felt no trace of pity for the mother who pleaded for her child, or for the old man staring in disbelief at the purple veil spread out over the smouldering ruins.

For years he continued in this self-directed nightmare. But one day, before the sack of Sokologbo, he was hiding behind a rock when some small boys came skipping down the path, waving bird-scarers to shoo the doves off the millet fields. He would never forget their gasps as the Amazons pounced from the bushes and garrotted them one by one.

All that morning, as the Dahomeans did their work, he buried his face in his hands, muttering, 'No. Not the children!' and never went to war again.

BUT THE KING became a warrior more frightful than any of his ancestors.

He broke Grito in 1818, Lozogohé in 1820 and Lemón in 1825. He killed Atobé of Mahi, Adafé of Napou and Achadé of Léfou-Léfou. He made the Atakpameans eat their fathers in a stew. He swore to defeat the Egbas in their stronghold at Abeokuta, and he told the Alafin of Oyo to 'eat parrots' eggs'.

He was not cruel. He too sickened at the sight of blood and would avert his eyes from the executions. He longed to end the cycles of war and revenge – yet he could never resist the temptation to acquire more skulls.

The skulls of his enemies assured him that he was alive

117

in the world of real things. He drank from skulls, he spat into skulls. Skulls formed the feet of his throne, the sides of his bed and the path that led to the bed-chamber. He knew the name of every skull in his Skull-House and held imaginary conversations with each in turn: the lesser enemies were piled on copper trays, but the great ones were wrapped in silk and kept in whitewashed baskets.

Not that he could have spared many victims had he wanted to. The war-commanders eyed him for the first sign of weakness, and a body of priests was always on hand to advise which captives should go to the Dead-land, and which to the Americas.

Dom Francisco would think up ways to save them from the knife: he found the best plan was to divert the nobles' attention with some novelty imported from Europe.

One year, when the palace architects were planning a skull-mosaic, he suggested using porcelain plates in-stead. At first, the King was overjoyed at the idea of 'breaking' such valuable property and dashed a whole pile to the ground. Then, as if he heard his ancestors growling, he frowned, his dead eye drained the light from the live one, and he barked out:

'War is for taking heads, not selling them attached to bodies.'

GRADUALLY THE TWO friends lost the art of communicat-ing except through presents. But though Dom Francisco's presents usually pleased the King, the King had nothing to offer but women – and such were his ideas of friendship that he posted spies inside the Fort at Ouidah to make sure each one was used.

The mistress of the seraglio was still Jijibou.

She had weathered the upheavals and grown into a big-jowled woman, shapely as a horse, with a satiny gloss to her skin. She spent her days in the shade of her hut, muffled in orange cloth, and was never seen to smile.

Her father, the kruman, had died. He drowned the day his canoe capsized and, even if Jijibou suspected her husband of selling him to a slaver, she did not allow her suspicions to interfere with her household duties.

She would inspect the girls to make sure they were virgins, calm their fears and lead them to the bedroom. She brought each new baby to its father, but their squalling only reminded him of his Brazilian child, and, as their tiny fingers clawed at his beard, he would grit his teeth and stop his ears and hurry off.

To uphold the decencies of the Church, he insisted on Christian baptism and made Jijibou go through a fiction of being the real mother. He tried to read her thoughts as she stood by the font. But if she caught him glancing in her direction, her eyes would narrow and the facets of her mouth turn down.

By 1835 THE size of his family had outgrown the Fort. So, work began on the mansion he had been cheated of building in Brazil.

Simbodji – which means 'Big House' in Fon – lay

119

open to Atlantic breezes on a sloping site between the King's Baobab and the Captains' Tree.

The house that emerged from its chrysalis of palm scaffolds was a replica of Tapuitapera except that, for want of stone foundations, it was unsafe to build a second storey. The pink walls were the same, the up-turned eaves, the blue dining-room, and the cross-lattice windows that were painted green.

The houseboys had never seen glass windows before, and when they saw the reflection of the setting sun, they thought they were ablaze and doused them with water.

Dom Francisco imported jacaranda couches, an opa-line toilet set, the Swiss musical boxes and the Goanese bed. A piano came from Germany. The billiard-table came through the surf on a raft of three canoes lashed together.

His own rooms were tall and cool, and stripes of sun-light filtered through the shutters. The verandah gave on to a garden of night-scented flowers, and there was a path that led through the wall to the seraglio.

Facing his bed, he hung up a panorama of Bahia, but the sight of it made him homesick and he replaced it with an engraving of the boy Emperor Dom Pedro II. His desk was stacked with old Brazilian newspapers. He tried to puzzle out the politics of the new Empire. The names meant nothing. He gave up and only read the advertise-ments.

One night, in a flash of inspiration, he wrote to Joaquim Coutinho, asking if the nuns of the Soledade could make a replica of the oratory of the Last Supper.

Joaquim, it so happened, was delighted at being spared the embarrassment of his partner's return. He lost no time in sending a crate with a letter:

My consort and I take pleasure in sending the original, with our blessings for the Christian community established at Ouidah . . .

A PORTRAIT OF Dom Francisco at the age of fifty would have shown a man strangely unaffected by the climate. A scar fanned out from his right temple. A deep furrow split his forehead into two. But his skin, though yellowish, was unwrinkled. His hair and beard were black and glossy, and he moved with the easy strides of youth.

He took not the slightest trouble with his clothes. By day he wore a planter's suit of grey calico, an old pair of boots and a bandless straw hat with holes in it. He would make his dinner guests wear freshly laundered whites, only to insult them by turning up in a dirty chintz housecoat and pantaloons that trailed over his Moorish slippers.

Not that he had no other clothes. In his bedroom was a wardrobe painted with Chinese landscapes, stuffed full of the clothes he ordered from the tailors of London and Paris for the receptions he would never attend. Some nights, behind a bolted door, he put on evening dress and would extend a white-gloved hand to the cheval-glass that flaked and pitted far faster than his own face. Then, when the moths and silverfish began their work, he would tell Taparica to burn the lot and write out fresh orders to his agent.

He wore no watch. He knew the time from the sun or the constellations; and even when the sky was overcast, he could peer into the darkness and say, 'Three hours left till dawn.'

Yet he kept a collection of watches in a leather box beneath the bed – gold fobs and half-hunters; watches with rock crystal dials, or painted with scenes of the Turkish harem. His favourites were the Swiss musical clocks; and when his women heard the tiny birds twittering under the mattress they thought they were the spirits singing.

He would wind them up before retiring, taking care to set each one to a different hour: he was so much obsessed with the passage of time.

There were other nights when he would take out his rings, putting on one after the other till his fingers were stiff with the wild light of emeralds.

Afterwards he would stare moodily at his bare hands and call out, 'Taparica! Soap and water!' Then he would lie in his nightshirt, waiting for the creak of boards on the verandah: on the bad nights, the game of breaking virgins was his only hope of consolation.

THE DA SILVA boys were allowed to play naked till the age of seven. After that, their father dressed them in whites, put them to sleep in a dormitory and sent them to the padre's schoolroom to learn how to read.

They were lively boys and they learned easily. They learned their catechism and the verses of Camoens, but most days they came back from their lessons with blank, bewildered faces.

Twenty years of mission work in Angola had given Father de Lessa the appearance of a bird of prey and biblical convictions on the subject of Blacks. He had the habit of conducting scripture lessons in the form of rhetorical questions:

'Can the Ethiopian change his skin?' he would shout. 'Or the leopard his spots?'

Was not black the colour of night? Of the Devil? Was not black skin the very mark of Cain?

Dom Francisco guessed what was wrong and, one morning, sat outside the schoolroom and listened to the padre's peroration. Then he poked his head through the window and said, 'But blacks believe the Devil is white.'

HIS ELDEST SON, Isidoro, was sent to Bahia to finish his studies with the Coutinho boys. The family now lived in a big white mansion on the cliffs overlooking the bay. But Isidoro's wildness – and African toilet habits – so terrorized the ladies of the household that his guardian packed him off to a gloomy seminary in the hills.

There, in classrooms reeking of incense, he learned to parse a Latin sentence wearing a white cassock emblazoned with a red cross. He would come back for the holidays sunk-eyed and flabby. His coughing fits reminded the Fathers of consumption and, finally, they sent him away for good.

Back in Bahia, he soon recovered his spirits in the bars and brothels of the Pelourinho.

'I have decided', Joaquim Coutinho wrote to his partner, 'to shut my eyes to your son's indecencies, since the only means I have of controlling them would be to hand him over to the civil authorities, which, as a guardian, I am loath to do.'

But when the young mulatto staggered into the house, drenched with blood and his clothes ripped to ribbons, he was thrown out and sent to lodge with a slave-broker in the Lower City.

JOAQUIM COUTINHO USED Isidoro's behaviour as an excuse to break up the partnership: by 1838 slave-trading was no longer an occupation for a Brazilian gentleman.

It had been a criminal offence for ten years. But though it flourished without prosecution, though the Southern coffee-planters were crying out for slaves, the business had got into the hands of Portuguese nouveaux riches, whose business methods made them highly unpopular.

Brazilian liberals hated slavery on moral grounds and the conservatives mistrusted it for practical ones: there were far too many Blacks in Brazil.

In 1835 a slave revolt had all but overwhelmed the city of Bahia. The leaders, it turned out, were a cabal of Muslim fanatics who had infiltrated the Black Christian Brotherhoods and declared a Holy War. But in fashionable society the name of Toussaint-Louverture was on everyone's lips, while at Court the Emperor's ministers were known to favour German immigrants over Africans.

APART FROM HIS ships, Joaquim Coutinho was the owner of ranches, a diamond mine, a bank, streets of town property, and he was thinking of building a railway. He had also set his heart on a title, lived in dread of compromising himself and was particularly sensitive to his nickname, 'Old Meat'.

On a visit to Rio he bribed the imperial chamberlains. Then he cut his old associates and sold his fleet. He built two churches in the Gothic style; he endowed a convent, put his name at the top of every subscription list – and, finally, he had his reward.

One evening at Simbodji, as Dom Francisco leafed through the latest copy of the *Jornal do Rio de Janeiro*, he read that the well-known Bahia financier and philanthropist had been created Baron of Paraíba. A line engraving showed a spade-bearded man, coffined in a frock-coat, with gold chains round his paunch and the Order of St Boniface round his neck.

'Not the boy I knew,' he said.

He decided to risk a letter of congratulation, though five months passed before the reply came – a curt note regretting that public and private pressures no longer allowed him to attend to the African trade.

THE NEW BARON of Paraíba did at least have the grace – or the self-interest – to find an agent in Bahia for his ex-colleague.

José de Paraízo was a Portuguese who had learned from the experience of exile the art of making himself indispensable. His first action was to rescue Isidoro da Silva from the gutter. He bought him a new set of clothes, and made him pose in them for his portrait. Then he sent him to Marseille as an apprentice to a shipping company.

He also excelled in finding things to keep the King of Dahomey amused. In the same consignment as the portrait, he sent some lustre-ware kettle-drums, a Noah's Ark and a barrel-organ that played the Psalms. Next, he bought up the costumes that were sold off by the Rio Opera to defray its costs; and for a season, the court functionaries of Abomey swanned about dressed as characters from Rossini's *Semiramide*.

Another time, perhaps as a joke, he sent the canvas of Judith and Holophernes, but Dom Francisco kept it back:

'These people', he wrote, 'have so little humour. His Majesty might not be amused.'

Nor was there any way of telling if the King was pleased with a present; for he would frown at each one and lift an eyebrow, as if to say, 'What have you kept back this time?'

All the serving girls at Simbodji were royal spies: whatever went on in the household the King was the first to know. So, when Dom Francisco bought for himself a

126

silver swan that gobbled up fishes to the airs of Bellini, it vanished overnight, only to be sent back from Abomey with the neck off, the mechanism overwound and a warning never again to send anything broken.

THE KING HAD no use for gold. Gold was the currency of his enemy, the King of Ashanti, whereas Dahomey used cowrie-shells that could neither be faked nor adulterated.

But the Cubans and Yankees who came to buy slaves in Ouidah always preferred to pay in gold: ingots, doubloons, louis d'or, napoleons, sovereigns and sometimes the coins of the Great Moghul. Dom Francisco kept his hoard in money barrels buried under the bedroom floor: it alarmed him terribly when the King commanded one of them to be taken up to Abomey.

The King peered at the coins, one after the other, and let them slide through his fingers. He learned the names of Louis Philippe, the Elector of Brandenburg, Tsar Paul and the young Queen Victoria. Then he rolled his eyes and threw the lot to the ground, snorting, 'I wouldn't let anyone walk off with my head,' and never spoke of gold again.

IN THE RAINY season of 1842 Father de Lessa went mad.

He would come into the schoolroom naked and mortify himself with a leather flail. Or he could be seen stalking round the Python Temple, in a mud-spattered soutane, shrieking, 'I will make this city desolate. I will smite the abominations.'

One Sunday, as he was preparing the sacrament for Mass, he found a python curled up in his vestments and staved its head in with the butt of his processional cross. The fetish priests hauled him out of the chapel and, by the time Dom Francisco had rescued him, he was out of his mind.

He kept seeing an animal called the Zoo.

The Zoo had the head of a monkey, a dog's body, leopard claws, and it would sprawl lecherously across his path and twitter like a bird.

Dom Francisco decided to ship him back to Bahia. But the Zoo was also in the sea; for when they strapped him aboard the canoe, he was still screaming, 'The Zoo! The Zoo!'

ABOUT THIS TIME Isidoro came back from France with the airs of a dandy and a head full of schemes for starting a palm-oil factory: by the 1840s the middle classes of Europe had discovered the blessings of *savon blanc de Provence*.

A Marseille trading company, Mm. Binet and Poncetton, sent a scout to report on the palm plantations of the Slave Coast: it was through Isidoro's help that a thin-lipped young man called Blaise Brue reoccupied the old French Fort of Saint-Louis-de-Grégoy.

Blaise Brue played an excellent game of boston and was a welcome dinner guest at Simbodji. It was he who suggested turning Ouidah into a French protectorate.

As for Dom Francisco, he jumped at the chance of making clean money in the oil trade. He put his entire workforce at the Frenchman's disposal, and they went into partnership. They unchoked old palmeries and they planted new ones. From distant villages women converged on the Fort with oil calabashes balanced on their heads. In the first season, four thousand barrels were rolled to the beach, and Dom Francisco was seen again to smile.

He smiled as the palm nuts ripened the colour of embers and he smiled to watch the glutinous yellow liquid rise to the surface of the vats. Often, he would turn to his sons and say:

'One day palm-oil will make us rich beyond the dreams of avarice.'

But the young mulattos were stranded in a limbo. They hated their father. They hated any kind of work and, having no outlet for their energies, turned sour and moody, stole from the storerooms, or took to drink and discovered the pleasures of the knife.

DOM FRANCISCO'S LOVE-AFFAIR with France reached a climax when Louis Philippe's second son, the Prince de Joinville, landed off the frigate *Belle-Poule* to inspect the French factory.

That night at dinner, he served a Château Margaux of

1811 and provided a silver tooth-pick holder in the form of a porcupine for each officer to take as a souvenir.

The Prince made everyone laugh by telling scandalous stories about the English when he went to fetch the body of Napoleon off St Helena. He discussed the problem of cooling champagne in the tropics and the origin of the expression *'Perfide Albion'*. Then he drew a pencil sketch of his host – the basis of all future portraits – and retired to bed in the Goanese four-poster.

Next morning, when he came to leave, the Da Silva boys shouted 'Vivas!' The girls garlanded him with frangipani; and, presenting him with a box of his best Havanas, Dom Francisco asked him to put in a good word with his brother-in-law, Dom Pedro of Brazil.

'I shall tell him everything,' the Prince said.

It came as a terrible shock when Blaise Brue got a message from his company in Marseille to drop his association with the infamous slaver.

'I am sorry, mon vieux,' – and that was all he had to say.

IN DESPAIR DOM Francisco turned to the British, hoping that if he helped them, they would help him in return.

When a Bristol barque went ashore four miles down the coast at Jacquin, he cleared the beach of looters and helped the crew salvage the cargo. He rescued a Methodist mission stranded at Lagos, and looked after Mrs McCalvert when her husband blew his brains out. He even entertained the Englishmen who came with Lord

Palmerston's draft treaty for abolishing the Slave Trade.

The first 'Englishman' to visit the King was a Freetown 'trouser black', the Reverend Tommy Crowder, who was forced to witness the annual sacrifices and came back scared out of his wits. He did, however, just manage to stammer out the greetings of the Great White Queen.

The King's reply, which the clergyman transcribed into a kind of English, asked after the Queen's health and that of 'His Daughters and His Sons and His Mother and His Grandmother'. It agreed that selling slaves was 'BAD'; that Brazilians were 'BAD PIPPLE ONLY WANT SLAVE FOR MONEY'; and that 'Him Queen' should send a man with a 'Big Head to hear King Palaver and write Book Palaver and same way King of Dahomey send messenger to Queen bye and bye'.

The man with a 'Big Head', Captain William Munro, arrived six months later in the uniform of the 1st Life Guards. He had ginger hair, candid blue eyes, a tuft of ginger whiskers on the bridge of his nose, and his conversation was full of the stock phrases of Abolitionist literature. He had brought the King a present of a pair of peacocks, and a spinning-wheel from his mother in the Highlands.

Over dinner he tried to convince Dom Francisco that the soil of Dahomey was ideal for growing cotton.

'Yes. Yes,' his host replied. 'It will come. It will all come. You will bring them railways and make them very happy. You may even stop them killing each other. But that will take a long time, and I am much too old and tired to try. All I can do, my dear young friend, is offer you the hospitality of my simple house.'

He was laid up with rheumatism the day the mission left for Abomey; but calling the Captain to his bedside, he gripped his hand and whispered, 'Do, please, commend me to the King.'

Afterwards, no one knew if the interpreter was to blame, or Munro's naivety, or the King's desire to please. But the Foreign Office got the impression that the King was a 'just and humane man', who longed to be rid of the 'detestable Da Silva' and take up the peaceful arts of agriculture.

In his turn, the King had the pleasing vision of an annual subsidy of three thousand pounds from his White Sister, which would allow him to make war and take as many heads as he liked without the troublesome business of selling captives.

His letter to Queen Victoria promised to expel all the slavers from Ouidah; and since the Queen's heart was a 'BIG CALABASH overflowing with palm-wine for the thirsty man', he needed a big tent and a golden carriage – now.

Three more English missions came, each worse-tempered than the last, and a Vice-Consulate was set up at Ouidah in the old British Fort.

The King promised one thing, then another, but never put his cross to the treaty. No tent came from England, nor did the golden carriage. Instead Consul Crosby took the King a suit of chain mail, some gutta-percha masks of Punch and Judy, a contraption called Dr Merryweather's Tempest Prognosticator, and a copy of the *Illustrated London News* covering the Great Exhibition.

The meanness of these presents shocked the King into asking Dom Francisco what three thousand pounds would pay for:

'Your household expenses for one week.'

The Vice-Consul was a sour-faced man, who held himself excessively erect and had cheeks that looked as if they were pumped full of grease. He earned Dom Francisco's undying hatred when he pointed at Taparica and said, 'I see, sir, that you keep a performing monkey.'

His orders from Lord Palmerston were to insist that Dahomey refrain from attacking the city of Abeokuta, where there were Anglican missionaries. The King, however, had promised his ancestors to leave Abeokuta a pile of ashes – and he promised the English nothing.

At his last audience, Crosby made the mistake of lecturing on the evils of war, at which the King produced a framed engraving of the Battle of Waterloo and said, 'Whose war, Mr Consul? Whose war?'

The Consul's reply was to present the King with a native hoe together with some comment about 'doing a useful job of work'. The King then flew into a rage, threw a necklet of bat wings in the envoy's face and bellowed, 'Take that for the old woman!'

Consul Crosby broke off negotiations and closed the Consulate.

The King went to war.

Two missionaries stationed at Abeokuta, Messrs Bickersteth and Smith, gave the Egbas lessons in arms drill and provided ammunition. On March 3rd 1851, five thousand Dahomeans were killed below the Sacred Rock. It was the worst defeat in their history.

The West Africa Squadron then blockaded the port of Ouidah and the King's ministers blamed Dom Francisco for letting the Englishmen into the country.

BUT WORSE TROUBLES were to come from the 'Brazilians'.

The first 'Brazilians' in Ouidah were a shipload of ex-slaves, who had bought their freedom and chartered an English merchantman to take them back to Africa. They landed near Lagos, hoping to go upcountry to their old homes in Oyo. But the fetid swamps were far from the paradise of their grandmothers' tales. Villagers stoned them and let loose their dogs. They panicked at the thought of being sold again. They were homesick for Brazil but, with one-way passports, had nowhere else to go.

Dom Francisco heard of their plight and sent his cutter to offer them asylum.

He met them on the beach, the men in stove-pipe hats, the women in white-lace crinolines with their hair ironed flat. He gave them parcels of land and soon their cheerful farms dotted the countryside all the way to Savi.

The 'Brazilians' turned Ouidah into a Little Brazil. They went on picnics. They gave dinners. They planted pots of love-lies-bleeding and the marvel of Peru. They decorated their rooms with pictures of St George and the Dragon and, at Carnaval, would pelt each other with waxed oranges full of scented water.

The whole town changed colour. Instead of dull pinks and ochres, the houses took on the hues of a Brazilian garden; and as the women leaned over their half-doors, they seemed to be wearing them as an extension of their dress.

On the hot days they would lounge on their balconies, fanning themselves or scratching their backs with ivory back-scratchers. Sometimes, a chain of captives came clanking by with dogs at their heels – and the 'Brazilians' would fling flowers into the street, shout *'Boa Viagem!'* and sigh for the great houses of Bahia and Pernambuco.

Every Saturday, Dom Francisco gave a dinner for the leaders of the colony. All of them agreed that Simbodji was gloomy, old-fashioned and vulgar.

THE NEWCOMERS WERE very fussy about their health and, for the first time, Ouidah had a doctor.

He was Dr Marcos Brandão Ferraez, a harassed young mulatto, gone grey at thirty, who could be seen hurrying on his rounds with a green carpet-bag. Back in Brazil he had eloped with a Sertanista from a small town in Ceará: they decided to go to Africa when her brothers threatened to kill him.

The couple were childless and lived in two neat rooms above their pharmacy, where they put a plaster bust of Hippocrates and rows of blue pottery drug jars inscribed with Latin names; and they had a macaw called Zé Piranha.

Dona Luciana kept a spotless kitchen. No one knew better how to make guava marmalade or stuff a crab. She sang as she pounded her spices and, when she sang, her upper lip lifted in an enchanting way. But they were all sad songs. She had sung them as a girl, when she ached to get out of the backlands – to which she was aching to return.

After a while, she seemed to shrivel away in the heat. Her hair hung in rat-tails and her face came up in a rash. She was terrified of going out, mistook scorpions for snakes and would sit, miserably fingering her crucifix, till her husband came back.

One midday, as Dom Francisco was walking home with Taparica, he stopped dead in his tracks. Clearly and slowly, through the pharmacy window, came the words of a song that untied knots in his memory. It was a song his mother sang, about the gipsy woman who walked from fair to fair; and when Dona Luciana came to the final stanza, he joined in the last two lines.

She froze.

He peered in.

She took one look under the brim of his hat, saw the eyes and afterwards swore she had seen the Devil.

ON THE OTHER hand he was always welcome for a glass of sweet lime at the house of Jacinto das Chagas, a half-Yoruba mulatto who had been a clerk on a sugar estate and had a lovely daughter called Venossa.

Jacinto's calm smile, his gentlemanly bearing, his temperance and clean cotton suits made a lasting impression on the Dahomeans. Years of deference had taught him how best to worm his way into another's confidence, or play on another's guilt. Whenever he spoke of the Slave Trade, he would splay his long bony fingers over his heart and sigh, 'My brothers! My poor black brothers!'

Because of his reliability, and his head for figures, Dom Francisco took him on as his assistant. He trusted him with commercial secrets he would never have shared with his sons. And he even trusted him on confidential errands to the King.

At first the King was infuriated by the idea of black men in shoes, but when Jacinto told him of the 'Brazilians' ' marriages in the chapel, he too said he needed a Christian bride: the whole colony was disgusted by Jacinto's decision to sacrifice his own daughter.

One drizzly morning, veiled so no one should see her crying, and driving her fingernails through a purse of blue satin, Venossa das Chagas said, 'I will,' between sobs; and she walked down the aisle on the arm of Dom Francisco, who stood proxy for his blood-brother in a black morning coat.

An Amazon guard of honour escorted her to Abomey where, forty-nine years later, a French army officer found her, bent double before a crucifix in an attitude of prayer.

It was she who ruined the Da Silvas.

A MONTH AFTER the marriage, her father picked a quarrel with his employer, made friends with the French, and set up as a palm-oil exporter on his own. The King gave him land and slaves. He built a house with white columns and filled it with furniture from Paris. Soon, under the cover of the oil business, he started selling slaves to dealers from the United States.

Dom Francisco heard his monopoly was broken, and thought he was going mad. He burst in on the Das Chagas family at luncheon and sneered:

'Where are your black brothers now?'

'Those were Mahis,' Jacinto replied, 'not my people.'

In message after message, Dom Francisco tried to get his rival expelled but Jacinto had taught the King the true value of gold. And he had hinted that half the Da Silvas' fortune was already in Brazil – a capital crime in a country where every scrap of property was royal.

Without warning the King's tax-collectors swarmed into Simbodji and removed all the silver and gold. A month later, a steam-frigate of the West Africa Squadron boarded the last Baltimore clipper: it was obvious that Jacinto had tipped the British off.

The women of Simbodji said, 'The Big Tree is falling,' for quite suddenly the master was old.

AND TAPARICA WAS dying.

His head drooped. His skin shrivelled and red crescents showed up under his eyeballs. Some days he peered like a lost child, not knowing where he was. When the end came, Dom Francisco would not let him die on a mat, laid him down on the Goanese bed and held his scaly hand through three suffocating nights.

The voice croaked through the curtains:

'You not know this people. You not learn them never.'

Taparica tried to explain the various kinds of poison

and their antidotes. But the seabird part of him had flown, back to his island in the Bay of Bahia, where he had once licked the armpit of the woman who had taught him the mysterious medicine of excrements.

Dom Francisco buried him at dawn in a grave among the flowerbeds. A clammy mist enveloped his private sorrow, and he stared at the mud-stained shroud.

From over the wall of the seraglio, he could hear the women wailing, but the wails sounded more like a song of triumph.

A WORRIED DR Brandão Ferraez appeared one morning before breakfast to report a case of yellow fever in a 'Brazilian' house where a girl had entertained a Cuban sailor.

Within a week groans and muffled prayers sounded in every street. The disease struck down hundreds of blacks and mulattos but left the whites alone. The 'Brazilians' hung purple cloths from their balconies and, if they strayed out of doors, tied sponges soaked in vinegar under their noses. Isidoro and his half-brother Antonio lit bonfires to stop the contagion, but the sparks set fire to a roof and burned down several houses.

Ten Da Silvas died of the disease; and the doctor was the last of its victims.

He came home from calling on a case, his cheeks concave and his eyes congested and yellow. He said, 'Don't touch me! Don't come near me!' and lay down on his bed.

By noon he was writhing on the floor with streams of

black vomit, black as coffee grounds, spilling from his lips. Towards evening there was a storm. The clouds were the colour of mud. The palms bent and hissed. For another hour he lay quietly. Then he screamed as if an arrow had pierced his throat, and he died.

In the crowd watching the body as it came feet first through the pharmacy door was a hysterical woman who had lost all her children. The second she saw Dona Luciana, she shrieked out, 'Witch!'

The mob smashed the drug jars and the bust of Hippocrates lay headless in the street.

Dom Francisco heard the pandemonium and guessed the cause. Half an hour later, he and the houseboy carried in a bundle of rags and clotted blood, which they set on the Goanese bed.

For ten days Dona Luciana wavered between life and death, though she ate greedily what food was put before her. When she was well enough to recognize her rescuer, she shut her mouth so tightly they had to feed her by force.

Whenever he came into the room, she would cringe like a nocturnal mammal brought into the sunlight. It took weeks for her to get used to his presence. Then, suddenly, overnight, the man who had been the Devil was transfigured into her Guardian Angel.

He took care not to touch her, not even to touch her sleeve or her hand. Yet, joining two miseries in one, they took comfort from each other's company and could not bear to be apart.

He let her live on at Simbodji. She slept in the bed, while he slept next door on one of the jacaranda couches. He had the door of the seraglio walled up, and they stayed indoors and saw no one.

140

They lived as a man and a wife who have sworn themselves to chastity. She made an altar table and put vases
of white flowers on either side of the oratory of the Last
Supper. She kept a candle burning, and she promised to
save his soul.

She would read from the New Testament the stories of
Christ's forgiveness for sinners, with the sunbeams falling over her widow's weeds and her chignon of flaxen
hair. Her neck was very white: around it, on a velvet
ribbon, hung a locket of her husband's curls.

Dom Francisco listened, while Zé Piranha perched on
his shoulder and poked his mandible into his ear: when
the macaw's feathers came out, he would stroke his
poll and say softly, 'Poor bird! He wants to go back
home.'

In the rainy season, his attacks of rheumatism got
worse and for weeks he would be too stiff to move. She
applied hot compresses to his spine: she knew any
number of remedies, but had lost her medicines in the
pharmacy fire.

The women of Simbodji hated their rival. Even in a
rainstorm, Jijibou would bang and bang on the door,
clamouring to be let in. She made such a row that Dom
Francisco had to send for Isidoro who calmed his mother
down and, for the first time, earned his father's gratitude.

Of all his children he cared only for two twin sisters by
a mulatto woman who had died. Their names were
Umbelina and Leocadia and they were growing up to be
beauties. Dona Luciana said, 'Let them come and live
with us. Twins will bring us luck,' and she gave them a
mother's love.

She sewed them frilly white dresses and tied satin

141

ribbons in their hair. She taught them to embroider their initials on handkerchiefs. Together they made a picture of the Virgin Mary, using Zé Piranha's moulting wing-feathers for the robe, and his breast for the halo. Often, they took a picnic to the Chinese pavilion at Zomai. All four of them would sing the songs of the Bandeirantes. And how the girls screamed when their father told the story of the Goblin-with-hair-for-hands!

On one of these picnics, Dona Luciana asked if he ever thought of going back to Brazil.

'If God wills it,' he said. 'I would give anything to die in my country.'

From that day onward she could think of nothing else. She was full of schemes for slipping past the King's guards, who now watched over them night and day. But he, the man of action, seemed incapable of action. He would press his fists against his temples and say, 'But how? How? How?'

But she knew there had to be a way.

He still owned property in Brazil – a cigar factory at Magarogipe, a ranch, a sawmill and a few town houses – which his agent had bought as an investment when the price of slaves was up. Not without misgivings, he wrote to José de Paraízo asking him to buy a house in Bahia for his retirement, begging him keep it a secret.

Six months later, together with a copy of the title deeds to No. 1 Beco do Corto, Barra, came a crudely painted canvas, still reeking of turpentine, with a pink villa in a garden going down to the sea.

Dona Luciana clapped her hands as they unwrapped it, and asked what were the squiggles in the sky.

'Birds,' he said.

The first half of Paraízo's letter listed the furniture and

the names of the household slaves: he had kept back the bad news for the end.

Because of an oversight by the Baron of Paraíba, Dom Francisco's citizenship had been allowed to lapse. The Governor of Bahia had turned down his petition for a passport. Slaving was now a criminal offence: they would arrest him the minute he landed.

And yet, Paraízo continued, perhaps there was no cause for alarm: a contribution to charity would surely solve the problem. Another year passed. But when the *Jornal da Bahia* reported the opening of the sailors' hospital, Dom Francisco read the text of the Baron's address – and not a mention of his name among the donors.

In letter after letter, Dona Luciana appealed to the Governor, to the Baron and even to the Emperor himself: if all failed they would travel to Rome and lay their case before the Apostle Nunciate.

In her imagination she saw the great golden church, the choirs, the angels and the sunlight slanting sideways on the altar. The smell of incense already tingled in her nostrils. Then a figure in shining white would get up from his throne, and raise his hand in benediction, and say, 'Rise, Francisco! Reborn in the body of our Saviour!'

THEY WENT ON waiting for news and there was none.

Umbelina and Leocadia were too frightened to go out. Their half-brothers would jeer them, push them against the wall, and pretend that they were wanted by the King. Their father feared for their safety. Firmly, he ordered

143

Dona Luciana to take them to the house in Bahia, where she would lobby for his pardon and he would, one day, join them.

The Da Silvas were overjoyed to see the back of her: her departure was a scene of jubilation. But when she saw the ship slewing in the swells, and the tears in his eyes, she threw her arms around his neck and said, 'No. I cannot go.'

The setting sun had coloured the waves a milky golden green. The canoes looked like giant black centipedes as the crews heaved them down the scarp of the beach. Gently, Dom Francisco disentangled the moaning girls and led them to the water's edge. He gave the Captain a note for the Baron of Paraíba, commending them to his care. Flecks of foam blew on to Dona Luciana's black taffeta dress. And they stood, arm in arm, on the sand, watching the brown arms waving from a wavecrest and falling into the trough beyond.

That night she accepted an old man's love.

Two months later, she felt faint and had a twinge of pain in her stomach. Not till she started to swell would she believe what her instincts told her: she had always believed herself to be barren.

The pregnancy was difficult – and dangerous for a woman in her forties. Yet after a painful struggle, on January 21st 1854, she gave birth to a daughter. The baby was sickly: they had her baptized in the bedroom in case she failed to live.

144

But Eugenia da Silva clung to life and greedily took the teat of her wetnurse, though, at the same time, her mother had daydreams of falling into a slimy pit.

Eventually, the pardon came – a sheet of paper signed by the Emperor himself, acknowledging Lieutenant da Silva's 'many years of zeal and useful service at the Fort of São Jõao Baptista da Ajuda'. In the first rush of excitement, they did not take in the contents of Paraízo's letter, with its catalogue of debts to the Banco Coutinho, the failure of the cigar factory, the disease that had killed his cattle, the landslide, and the decision of the Bahia Society of Commerce to declare him bankrupt.

He said, 'They have robbed me,' and let fall the sheet of paper.

HE WROTE, FOR the last time, to the Baron of Paraíba:

Please, my dear friend, be patient with me. I would give you all I possess in Bahia. But what would people say? Everyone would turn against me if they knew I had nothing. They would say I could no longer count on you, my most trusted friend and protector over all these years. I ask you, I implore you, not to sell my furniture or my slaves, but put the house out to rent, so that my life may not be criticized. And I beg of you take care of my daughters . . . '

The Baron did not reply to this letter. His bank foreclosed the mortgage. The bailiffs carted off the furniture, and the house and slaves were sold, unadvertised, at public auction. There was one bidder, Senhor Ricardo Paraízo, the agent's brother, who opened the place as an academy for young ladies.

But Umbelina and Leocadia did not attend classes at that school, or at any other school. They did not live in the Coutinho household, even as servants. Instead, they were sent to a famous personality called Mãe Andresinha, who taught them a trade on the cobbles of the Pelourinho.

'Whores?' their father howled at the captain, who told him that news. 'Whores? My darling daughters? Whores?' And he set his fists on the table and watched his whitening knuckles, and he choked with sobs.

ON THE NIGHT of February 15th 1855, disguised as masked carnival dancers, he and Dona Luciana tried to smuggle themselves and their baby aboard a Brazilian ship. The night was cloudy, but the moon came out as they crossed the lagoon, and the sentries brought them back, as prisoners, to Simbodji.

Dom Francisco was stripped of his wealth and privileges though he was allowed to live on in rooms bare of all but the bed. He was the King's blood-brother: it was a crime to touch a hair on his head, yet even his own sons spoke of him in the past tense.

On the hot days, he would lie in the shade of a mango and let little Eugenia clamber over his belly and tug at his beard. His eyes were weak. His hands weighed heavily under a network of grey veins.

He would shred the petals of a rose or bury his face in a hibiscus flower. If his old gardener passed by, he would open his mouth to bark an order, but no words came. Or he would listen to the howling of the surf, and bang his head against the wall. At night, he saw rows of bloodshot eyes glaring at him out of the darkness.

Some nights he lay under the tree till dawn and, by morning, the snails had left silvery threads over his legs. On tatters of paper, he scribbled incoherent prophecies, which Isidoro had his houseboys collect in case they contained information about the Brazilian fortune:

> In 1860 the thorns will bear fruit but there will be few heads on bodies. – In 1870 there will be no heads to fill the hats. – In 1880 the slaves will sell their masters and buy wings. – In 1890 the Emperor will send a ship for his friend, but the sea will run red and the sky will turn to mud. And there will be a rain of stars and the ship will sink. – In 1900 the Holy House of Rome will crumble and bodies will choke the streets of Bahia and Jerusalem.

And Dona Luciana was sick and could do nothing to help him.

SHE HAD A bitter taste in her mouth and headaches so terrible that the sutures of her skull seemed to crack. She said, 'It's nothing. It must be the clouds. If only the clouds would go away.' She tried to smile, but the strain of forcing a smile made the pain much worse.

147

Then the skin flaked off her arms and legs, and left humid patches covered with a mouldering blush. Then her toes went numb, and her fingers, and the patches of skin turned black.

She could hardly breathe. Giddily, and with her pupils distended, she would gasp to Eugenia's wetnurse, 'Wash my arms! Look! Look! The spots are eating my arms!' Or in bursts of euphoria, she would cling to the bedposts, and bare her gums and chant Alleluias! at the top of her voice.

One morning, he saw threads of dark green mucus trailing from her mouth. Dimly, he remembered Taparica's dying words and murmured, 'Poison!'

She said, 'I'm so tired,' as she passed into a coma.

HE CLUNG TO the body, but the grave-diggers tore him away and he flapped his arms and cawed like a wounded bird.

He never saw the smile of triumph spread over Jijibou's shining face. He had run off into the canebrakes and went missing for days. Search-parties failed to find him. Then a man coming home from his yam-patch saw something blue in the undergrowth. Brushing the branches aside, he made out a matt-haired figure on all fours, with a big bird perching on its shoulder.

Zé Piranha bit Isidoro's hand when they came for his master. But they overpowered the old man and chained him to a tree beside the Chinese pavilion at Zomai. Only later, when the rage went out of him, did they let him wander freely round the town.

He would hobble round Simbodji crying, 'My daughters! What have they done with my darling daughters?' But the women hid little Eugenia so she should not see her father.

One woman gave her a wooden doll and, at sunset, she would lay it down, wrap it in a scarf, stroke the tippet of white fur stuck to its chin, and whisper, 'Sleep, Papa! Sleep!'

With rags falling off his body, he would skulk round the Legba Fetish. Only when no one was looking would he filch the offerings of cowrie-shells and buy himself a mouthful of food. He never ate Jijibou's scraps for fear that they were poisoned.

He talked to the waves on the beach. He even threw himself to the waves, but the waves threw him back; and they found him, bitten raw by sandflies and the crabs crawling over his body.

Gasping for water one day, he saw the King come towards him, smiling and showing the gap between his two front teeth. The King was young again, and was wearing his pink hunting costume. He laid a cool hand on his old friend's forehead and unstoppered his watergourd.

Dom Francisco reached out both hands to receive it, only to wake and see the black pig snuffling round his toes.

March 8th 1857 was a white-hot day with the wind kicking up dust-devils in the street. Dressed in their best black frock-coats, Isidoro da Silva and his brothers were giving a luncheon to thank Jacinto das Chagas for smoothing out their problems with the King.

Dragging his left leg, Dom Francisco came through the Brazil Quarter, mobbed by a gang of boys chanting, '*Bom*

Dia, Yovo! Yovo, Bom Dia!' and making the sign of the knife.

There were scabs on his kneecaps.

He passed the plaster elephant over the front gate. He limped over to the gaming saloon, where some of his Swiss musical boxes lay undisturbed on a table. And he wound them up, one after the other, till the room was bursting with random sound.

The door of the dining room opened and his sons stood before him. He peered at the faces filling the doorway. Some of them had napkins tucked into their collars. Jacinto excused himself and slipped away.

The old man was crying. Tears sped down the creases of his cheeks, only to be sopped up in the mud that had caked in his beard. He opened his mouth to speak, but his lower lip hung slack, and the music whirled, round and round his skull, as he reeled from the room, out into the light and dust and hawks and dark and nothing.

SIX

THIS IS WHAT Mama Wéwé remembered as she lay dying:

She remembered the rags, the scabbed legs and the swift, spiralling shadows on the ground. The women were wailing and there was an odour of burning. They burned the crops and the canebrakes. They set the chairs on the table, so there would be no place for the old man's soul to sit – for once he sat down, he would sit there for ever.

She never knew if she remembered – or if they told her later – of the King's great grief: blood-brothers go together when they go to the Big House. Perhaps he knew that he would die within the year.

Or the Amazons howling. 'No. No. No. It was not the leopard that killed him. Not the buffalo that killed him. It was Night. Night that killed him!'

But she could see clearly again the mourners carrying goats and chickens; the grave-digger shovelling spadefuls of soil through the bedroom window; and the rum barrel – it was Antonio's idea to bury him in a rum barrel; and the shaved white head with wads of kapok stuffed up the nostrils.

Once again, they were all around her, the cringing men and the set, fanatic faces of the women: it was not to be a Christian funeral.

Again hands lifted her for one last look – at the head bobbing in the barrel and the boy and girl standing beside it, whimpering. They put her down when the sacrificer came with a knife.

Then she was running, faster and faster down a wet red tunnel with no light at the end. A door opened. A cool draught blew in her face. A mulatto in a white suit brushed past her, turning his face to the wall.

And she stepped into a tall blue room lined with mirrors and pillars of gold. A dinner-party was ending. A man rose from the head of the table. He had red hair and his eyes were the colour of the market-women's beads. And he held out both his hands and said, 'I have waited a long time.'

LIEUTENANT-COLONEL ZOSSOUNGBO PATRICE heard the screams from his office in the Sûreté Nationale. His fatigues were drenched with sweat. He stopped composing his list of possible traitors. The President was coming to the end of his broadcast:

Victory to the People!
Glory to the People!
Power to the People!
Ready for the Revolution!
Ready for Production!
And the fight continues!

Fixed to the wall were a pair of handcuffs and a broken guitar. There was also a stuffed civet cat, nailed, in mockery of the Crucifixion, with its hind legs and tail together and its forelegs stretched apart.

Above the desk hung the scarified face of the President.

The colonel got up and made a gesture which, if any-one had seen it, would have landed him in jail.

Then he paced up and down, waving to an imaginary crowd, creaking the floorboards and crushing a cock-roach under the heel of his combat boot.

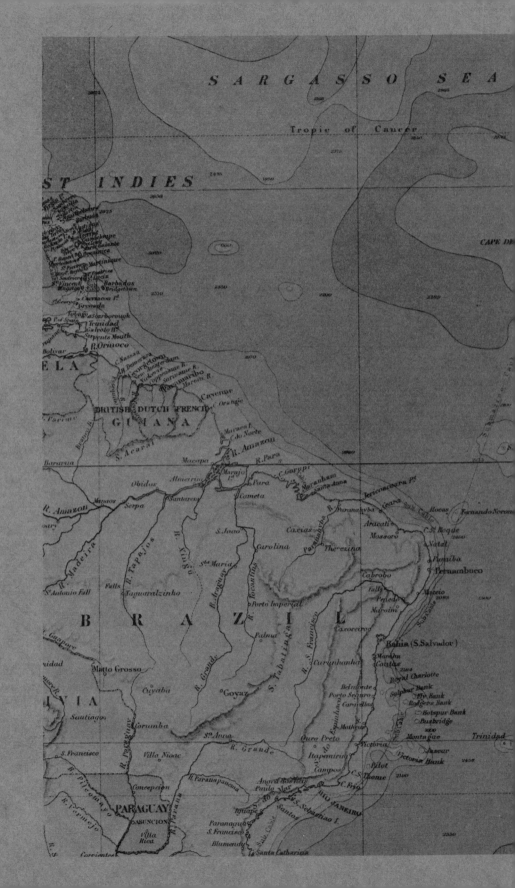